Aroma

THERAPY FOR LOST HUMANITY

LYNETTE JOHNSON

WESTBOW
P R E S S®
A DIVISION OF THOMAS NELSON
& ZONDERVAN

WestBow Press books may be ordered through booksellers or by contacting:

WestBow Press
A Division of Thomas Nelson & Zondervan
1663 Liberty Drive
Bloomington, IN 47403
www.westbowpress.com
844-714-3454

ISBN: 978-1-6642-2891-7 (sc)
ISBN: 978-1-6642-2890-0 (e)

Print information available on the last page.

WestBow Press rev. date: 05/07/2021

CONTENTS

PREFACE

History is paramount!

Growing up in Detroit Michigan, most of my education was through the Detroit Independent School District. One of my least favorite subjects was history. It did not matter whether the topic was local, State, American or World history, it was all boring. I was well in years when I developed an appreciation for history. It was like a light bulb came on, my eyes were opened and I realizing the true significance of understanding history.

Individuals who understand history receives a jump start into revelation of basic concepts and ideas. Light is being shed on the thoughts and beliefs of man during a certain dispensation in time. Enabling one to learn about cause and effect, relationships, and human nature.

Enough knowledge about history, can disclose how attitudes and feelings are affected as a result of a single action. History helps us to understand why things are the way they are today. Many past events in this world have shaped our present-day existence. Understanding what has happened, and looking closely at day-to-day happenings, enables one to predict the possibility of what may befall us in times to come.

In (Ecclesiastes 1:9 NIV) King Solomon declares that "The things that hath been, it is that which shall be: and that which is done is that which shall be done: and there is no new thing under the sun." Examining the past gives us a better outlook on the things we should avoid, help us to see what can be done presently and how to make things better in the future. Applying lessons learned from history, enable us to make needed changes to better our way of life.

Each of us are a part of history. We are impacting lives right now. What one does today may influence the history of the family for generations to come. And because we are a world of families; we have a part to play in the condition of our world. We can choose to be a part of the solution or part of the problem.

History does not stop at textbooks; it continues until the end of time. And each one of us is a living compilation of what is to come".

(http://EzineArticles.com/?What-Is-The –Importance o-Of-History)

As we journey into Noah's time, we see the destruction of nearly all living things. Noah, his family, and the animals on the Ark were the only survivors. What lead to such a catastrophe? Why was Noah and his family saved? And what does that have to do with me? These questions will be a source of serious discussion as we proceed through the pages of this book.

Carefully investigating the life of Noah; will bring about an awareness of the danger of history repeating itself.

One man chose to live in a way that pleased the Almighty God, in a time when the world chose to please themselves. The world's consequence was deadly.

With all the chaos in our world, we would do well to examine the history of Noah's time.

What can we do to make this world a better place? We look at the vastness of the world's ills and think, there is nothing I can do to change things, I am just one person. But there is something we can do. We can follow the guidelines the creator has set for all humanity. His governing blueprint for our life is to love God and each other. Loving God causes one to keep and obey his commandments. And the father promised to love us and make himself known unto us. Believers are the recipients of his peace, and promise in this chaotic world. We must do our part to prepare humanity for a soon coming king.

The scripture sheds light on the problem of men in Noah's day and our problem today. "Their minds are full of darkness; they wander far from the life God gives because they have closed their minds and hardened their hearts against him." (Ephesians 4:18 NLT) Why does humanity not whole heartedly search for God? The answer stems in humanism.

"Humanism is a belief that human needs and values are more important than religious beliefs. They believe that a person creates their own set of ethics." (www.your dictionary.com / humanism)

"Humanists believe human experience and rational thinking provide the only source of both knowledge and a moral code to live by. They reject the idea of knowledge 'revealed' by God or in special books."

(www.bbc.co.uk>religion>religions>atheism>types)

"Throughout history God's children had to resist the influence of the world (humanistic society) around them. Choosing to reject worldly values to walk close to God. Obeying Him and learning to think like He thinks. As believers we have to guard against wrong influences and values that separate us from God. We must guard our thinking and way of life."

(UCG.org Humanism: Dangerous Modern Philosophy with Ancient Origin)

The church is the light in this world's darkness. Lost humanity needs the light of Jesus Christ, shining through the church to experience life. It is only through the repentance of the church that we can receive true revival.

In the book of 2 Chronicles seventh chapter, God was conversing with Solomon concerning the answer to his prayer. Solomon wanted to know; if the people of God sinned and repented would they be forgiven. The Lord told Solomon that "if His people would humble themselves, pray, search for Him, and turn from their evil ways, He will hear their prayer, forgive their sins, and heal their country." (2 Chronicles 7:14 GW)

It is imperative that we as believers not fall asleep in these dangerous times. Matthew compared the "coming of the Son of Man to the days of Noah. In Noah's time before the flood, everyone was carrying on as usual, having a good time right up until the time that Noah boarded the Ark. They didn't know or understand what was going on until the flood came and swept them all away." (Matt. 24:37-39 AMP)

As long as there is life, we have time to cleanse ourselves with the Word of God. We have time to "present our bodies to God as a living sacrifice; holy and acceptable." (Romans12:1 KJV) The world needs the church to make a bold stand for the kingdom of God.

This book is designed to stir the faith of believers. And ignite a righteous fight within us to draw closer to God. The worlds condition is chaotic, and the actions of the visible church seemingly has conformed to the world. I pray that we will be inspired to be part of history that will cause men, women and children to want to know our Lord and Savior Jesus Christ.

Endeavoring to be a pleasant and agreeable odor to God and humanity.

INTRODUCTION

What does one really know about their parents?

I started writing this book to give my children some insight into my heart and character of the God I serve. It grew into something much bigger than I had anticipated.

Sometimes we are oblivious to why we are born, what is our purpose and how to find real meaning in life. Some may think, you are just a product of your environment. You and I are so much more.

Finding your purpose is finding your creator! It means living in accordance with the design of the one who was responsible for your existence. Real meaning in life, is learning how to live in a way that is a pleasing aroma to God. What does that really mean?

Being a pleasing aroma means having a God experience. The spirit of God comes into your life, makes himself known and leaves an imprint on your heart. This enables one to begin a lifelong journey with the Lord, learning to take on the character of their creator.

God initiates this experience and faith of the recipient brings about the beginning of a wonderful relationship. This life is lived by the help and power of the Holy Spirit. Fiery trials burn off the Adamic nature to further shape one into the image of Christ. (1Peter 4:12; 2 Cor. 4:8-10 KJV) Allowing this relationship to grow means obedience to God's will. In turn it will bring about joy in the heart of the believer. It is like one inhaling a pleasant scent and being overcome with a feeling of blissfulness.

God is love! So the adversary tries to snuff out any resemblance of God in the earth. Therefore we see an increase in sin. Mankind's love for one another has waxed cold. In order for change to happen in our world, God must be released. This takes place when earthen vessels (believer) allow the power of God in us to work spiritual life in others. "He is able to do exceeding, abundantly above all that we ask or think according to the power (the spirit of God) that is at work in the believer." (Eph. 3:20 KJV)

So as you proceed through these pages, you will learn a little about me, some about history, and hopefully more about your heavenly father, and his great plan for your life.

Most things in our environment, have a scent. Some scents are pleasant, and some are not. Some make you smile, and some make you frown. Some give a since of joy and your senses want more. While others make you want to get away as fast as you can. Some scents can even make you cry. And some are changed by applying other scents, like oils from flowers to water. Each scent has distinguishing traits that affect the surrounding atmosphere with aura. And everyone present is a receptacle of its power.

Pleasant fragrances like colognes and perfumes, can cause others to want to purchase them. So, they begin to inquire: What is the name of that perfume? Where can I find it? and How much did it cost? As that aura permeates the atmosphere someone will buy it for themselves. That is called advertising or promoting. Some people are so gifted and trained in the art of olfactory that they can tell what kind of fragrance an individual is wearing. In many cases they can even select the fragrance that best complement one's body chemistry. This is known as discernment. Believers should be promoters and discerners. The basic principles of marketing can be applied spiritually.

Transferring the goods of the producer (the love of God) to (humanity) the buyer. It is our responsibility to promote Christ; so that men can see beyond the replica and buy into the true aroma of an obedient life. We should be able to discern where one may be on their spiritual journey. And by chance help them to learn more of Christ.

When we look at the church today, it appears that many have lost the reality of God and settled for religiosity.

The Holy Spirit wants to encourage the body of Christ to be sensitive to the scent we are releasing before God. And make necessary changes, so others will want to buy into the Kingdom of God. Just as we smell things and are affected by them, God knows what comes from our heart, and it concerns Him. He is either pleased or displeased. I came to understand that our actions, attitude, and motives releases an odor (spiritually) from our hearts. God said in: (Jeremiah 17:10 KJV) "I the Lord search the heart, I try the reins, even to give every man according to his ways, and according to the fruit of his doings." Jesus said "whatever [word] comes out of the mouth comes from the heart, and this is what defiles and dishonors the man." (Matt. 15:18 AMP)

You may have heard someone use an idiom to describe a person's attitude or actions; for example, "her attitude stinks" or "he came out smelling like a rose".

Because we are connected to each other, we influence one another. In position of leadership, we have the power to impact a person's character. Leaders must be careful what we are promoting. The world as well as the church can discern if one has the true aroma of Christ.

In his dispensation, Noah was the prime example of a godly man. We can see despite the evil of his time he believed God and honored him to the point that he was a sweet Savor to the Lord. "Then Noah built an altar to honor the Lord. Noah took some of all the clean birds and some of all the clean animals and burned them on the altar as a gift to

God. The Lord smelled these sacrifices, and it pleased him." (Genesis 8:20-21a ERV) What did God smell by Noah's actions?

I believe that God got a whiff of faith and humility, that honored Him. And I can see in my Holy Ghost imagination that God smiled.

It is my prayer that we will be encouraged, enlightened and motivate by the Holy Spirit to make God smile. He is still looking for that pleasing aroma, that he may extend mercy and grace to our families and our world.

DEDICATION

To my mother and father-in-love Mother Willie Mae and Deacon Roosevelt Johnson Sr., who were my first examples of a godly aroma. Mother Johnson's love for The Lord and her kindness to me started me on my journey with God.

To my father and mother in the Gospel, Bishop Frank E. and Mother Thelma Johnson, who were responsible for my foundation and stability in Christ. They are great examples of God's love for His people.

To my husband Joseph, the love of my life, who believes in me and allowed me the time to put into words what The Lord had laid on my heart.

To my children: Reginald, Jibri, Anthony, Demetrius, Keyona, Latesha, Jonathan and Katrina whom I love dearly. To all my grandchildren, you have my deepest affection.

To all the wonderful people who God has placed in my life to help shape me into the person I am today. Thank you!

PART ONE

The Mix

WRONG IS WRONG
EVEN IF EVERYONE IS DOING IT

RIGHT IS RIGHT
EVEN IF NO ONE IS DOING IT – Pinterest

"Can both fresh water and saltwater flow from the same spring?
My brothers and sisters, can a fig tree bear olives, or a grapevine
bear figs? Neither can a salt spring produce
fresh water" James 3:11-12 NIV

THE DILEMMA

"The sons of God saw that daughters of men we're fair and they took wives of all they desired and chose." (Gen. 6:2 AMP)

"History repeats itself!" (In its original form it reads) "Those who cannot remember the past are condemned to repeat it." (George Santayana)

The book of Genesis gives us necessary information for understanding the meaning of human life and history. Some valuable insights are: The whole of creation owes its existence to God. Human evil stems from the first humans refusal to obey the Creator. And God kept alive the knowledge of truth and rightness by separating one man and his descendants from the rest of corrupted humanity. (Fire Bible book of Genesis Survey pg. 27; chapter 1:1 notes pg. 29)

At times, the sins of the parents are passed down to the children and beyond. These sins are called: generational curses. These curses are said to be defilements that are passed down from one generation to another. The concept of generational curses comes from the second of the Ten Commandments in (Exodus 20:4-6 HCSB.) "Do not make an idol for yourself, whether in the shape of anything in the heavens above or on the earth below or in the waters under the earth. You must not bow down to them or worship them; for I, the Lord your God, am a jealous God, punishing the children for the fathers' sin, to the third and fourth generations of those who hate Me. But showing faithful love to a thousand generations of those who love Me and keep My commands." We see in the book of Genesis that the sin of rebellion from Adam and Eve reared its ugly head in their son Cain. From the beginning of the history of man, God expected obedience from his creation.

Faith and obedience were the principles that would govern Adam's relationship with God. Adam was warned, if he rebelled against God's will, he would die.

God gave specific orders not to eat from the tree of knowledge of good and evil. As long as Adam obeyed, he would experience fellowship with God. But if he were disobedient, he would face the consequence of death. He would experience a separation from God, and at some point, undergo a natural death.

The Bible speaks of three kinds of deaths; physical death, the separation of body and spirit (the way of all mankind); spiritual death, (separation of individuals from God); and eternal death, and the final estate of the lost person in the "lake of fire" called the second death," (separation from God forever). (Rev.20:10,14 KJV) Thank God for eternal life through Jesus Christ. (1 Corinthians 15:55-57 KJV)

"O death where is thy sting? O grave, where is thy victory? The sting of death is sin; and the strength of sin is the law. But thanks be to God, which giveth us the victory through our Lord Jesus Christ." Because Jesus fulfilled the Law on our behalf by giving his life and winning forgiveness for our sins; death no longer has a stinging punishment, but victory of eternal life. When the believer receives their new body, they put on immortality, the final and complete victory over death.

My mother, Johnnie Mae Morant was diagnosed with lung cancer in April of 1978. She had been a smoker most of her life and did not accept Christ until she became ill. My husband petitioned for her to be his military dependent in the Air Force; and she was granted full military benefits. In the end of March we took my mother to the hospital, after she was having difficulty breathing. She was examined and was diagnosed with a common cold. When there was no improvement, we took her back. And was told she had pneumonia. It was not until my husband insisted that they run further test, it was discovered that she had a rare lung cancer. My mother passed away on July 2, 1978 peacefully to meet her Savior. Her body was buried in the ground, but her spirit went to be with the Lord. She chose in her later end to make Jesus her Lord and Savior. Thank God she had that chance!

The process of my mother's illness was difficult for us. Mom and I were remarkably close. I am the baby in the family and the only living sibling out of two brothers and two sisters.

Joseph and I had two children at the time and Jibri (my second oldest) was a baby. Mom couldn't do much for herself, so we had to bathe her and help her to the potty chair. She was blessed to eat on her own. We didn't know about hiring a caregiver, neither could we afford to pay for one, but the Lord gave us strength.

As her time of transitioning drew near, I felt I would grieve myself to death, if there is such a thing. I entreated the Lord to take the grief from me and he did. It was Sunday morning around 2:00 a.m. on July 2nd when we took my mother to the hospital. I remember asking her was she in any pain, and she was not. While we were sitting there, we dozed off to sleep. I was sitting in a chair next to the bed and my husband was sitting on a milk crate behind me. All of a sudden, I felt a slap on my leg, which woke me. There was no one in the room except my husband, myself and my mother. Turning around I asked Joseph did he hit me, he replied, "no." The only reasoning I could make out of it was that I needed to spend the last fleeting moments with my mother because the Lord was getting ready to take her. It was about 10:00 a.m. when our pastor Elder Frank Johnson came and had prayer with mom. A short time later some of the church members came into the room. Our friends Barbara and Foster were among them and persuaded us to go home with them to get something to eat. The pastor's sister stayed and promised to notify us if there was any change. A few hours had passed when the phone rang. It was the pastor's sister, letting us know that my mother had passed. When we arrived at the hospital we went straight to the room where my mother's body was. Grief struck me briefly, as if there was anticipation of a slap coming, and bracing myself for the sting, the hand stopped just shy of the face. But the anticipation was so strong that tears rolled down the cheek. When I saw my mother laying in that bed the tears begin to flow, but miraculously the Lord dried the tears and took the grief. "Surely he hath borne our griefs, and carried our sorrows:" (Isaiah 53:4a KJV) I appreciate the Lord for his faithfulness.

"But if serving the Lord seems undesirable to you, then choose for yourselves this day whom you will serve" (Joshua 24:15 NIV)

Adam had a choice: trust God and obey or doubt and rebel. He chose to defy God. The consequence was broken fellowship with his creator. Cursed and put out of the garden, judgement came upon them. Adam would work strenuously, and Eve would bear children in pain.

Adam and Eve's sin showed up in their son Cain, the first son of their procreation. Later Eve gave birth to her second son, Abel.

Abel was a Shepherd and Cain was a farmer. During the course of time the two brothers brought gifts to God. "Cain brought to the Lord and offering of the fruit of the ground. Abel' brought [an offering of] the [finest] firstborn of his flock and the fat portions. And the Lord had respect (regard) for Abel and for his offering; but for Cain and his offering He had no respect. Cain became extremely angry, attacked his brother and killed him." (Gen. 4:3-5,8 AMP)

Abel chose to give God his best and was praised for being a true worshiper. Such grace was made available to him due to faith and dedication to God, which was seen in his presentation. And because of this, God commended him for doing what was right. He became the first martyr, killed for his faith. On the other hand, Cain's heart lacked faith, and he selfishly chose what was wrong. He was jealous of his brother for receiving God's favor and angry with God for favoring Abel's offering. Judgement came upon Cain. There is a saying: jealousy is cruel as the grave. (Song of Solomon 8:6 KJV) And we see that Cain's jealousy drove him to murder his brother. So, God cursed the ground that he would cultivate; it would no longer yield good crops. Cain was therefore banished from the presence of God.

(Gen.4:4-10; Heb. 11:4 NIV) reference from Fire Bible study notes)

THE SEED OF EVIL

"Ah sinful nation, a people laden with iniquity, a seed of evildoers, children that are corrupters: they have forsaken the Lord, they have provoked the Holy One of Israel unto anger, they are gone away backward." (Isaiah 1:4 KJV)

Cain's attitude toward his offering to God and the subsequent murder of his brother caused him to be exiled from the presence of God. His decision not only effected himself, but it caused the seed of evil to be multiplied.

Cain was faced with a dilemma like his father. And humanity is faced with the same; do right or wrong, say yes or no, choose good or evil. And he chose evil.

It is always evil to disregard God's will and promote our own.

Making judgments according to ones fleshly desires and emotions, will breed corruption. It will not only have an effect on you but also on others.

God who knows everything begin to deal with Cain. "Why are you angry" God asked. "If you do what is right, will you not be accepted?

But if you do what is wrong, sin is crouching at your door; it desires to have you, but you must rule over it." (Gen. 4:7 NIV)

God describes sin as the enemy, who is lurking at the believer's door like a hungry animal, anticipating our destruction. Those who trust in God, are granted the ability to overcome the temptation of sin. The determination to yield to His plan and depend on his word guides us to victory.

Peter puts it this way: "Be sober [well balanced and self-disciplined], be alert and cautious at all times. That enemy of yours, the devil, prowls around like a roaring lion [fiercely hungry], seeking someone to devour. But resist him, be firm in your faith [against his attack – rooted, established, immovable], knowing that the same experiences of suffering are being experienced by your brother and sister throughout the world, [You do not suffer alone.] After you have suffered for a little while, the God of all grace [who imparts His blessing and favor], who called you to His own eternal glory in Christ, will Himself complete, confirm, strengthen, and establish you [making you what you ought to be]. To Him be dominion (power, authority, sovereignty) forever and ever. Amen." (1 Peter 5:8-11 AMP)

Apparently, Cain decided not to humble himself and repent to God. We see in (Genesis 4:16 NIV), that he separated "from the presence of God and lived in the land of Nod." He attempted to live without the help of the Lord. Cain's ungodly family increased in their self-reliance and centered their lives on the physical world's art and business.

Jesus said in Matthew twelve and thirty: "He who is not with me is against me, and he who does not gather with me scatters." (Matthew 12:30 NIV)

George Orwell: a British novelist, essayist, journalist and critic wrote.

An essay in 1942 entitled: "Pacifism and the War", which reads as such, "If you hamper the war effort of one side you automatically help that of the other. Nor is there any real way of remaining outside such a war as the present one. In practice, he that is not with me is against me."

So then, it matters not what one says but what one does, there is no neutral ground. Cain proved by his actions that he was not with God. If one does not honor God, and obey Him, their actions show that they are against Him.

Despite his actions, God was still merciful to Cain. He put a mark on him so no one would kill him for taking his brother's life. If they would attempt to do so their punishment would be seven times worse than Cain's. The established penalty for murder came later when wickedness and violence became extreme, and the Lord decided to destroy mankind for their unchanging evil. (Genesis 4:15 NIV)

The choice is still the same; do right or do wrong. One will experience consequences for their doings. So choose to do right!

"A good tree does not produce bad fruit. And a bad tree does not produce good fruit. Every tree is known by the kind of fruit it produces. You will not find figs on thorny weeds. And you cannot pick grapes from thorn bushes! Good people have good things in their hearts. That's why they say good things. But those who are evil have hearts full of evil, and that's why they say evil things. What people say with their mouths comes from what fills their hearts." (Luke 6:43-45 ERV)

The Apostle Paul declared: "I know that nothing good lives in me – I mean nothing good lives in the part of me that is not spiritual. I want to do what is good, but I don't do it. I don't do the good that I want to do. I do the evil that I don't want to do. So, if I do what I don't want to do, then I am not really the one doing it. It is the sin living in me that does it."(Romans 7:18-20 ERV)

As he examines his fleshly nature further, he says: "What a miserable person I am! Who will save me from this body that brings me death? I thank God for his salvation through Jesus Christ our Lord!" (Romans 7:24-25 ERV)

"Everyone who believes in Jesus will have their sins forgiven through his name. All the prophets agree that this is true." (Acts 10:40 ERV)

John talks about the love and sonship, those who believe in Jesus would receive. "Behold, what manner of love the Father hath bestowed upon us, that we should be called the sons of God: therefore, the world knoweth us not, because it knew him not." (1John 3:1KJV)

How wonderful it is to know the love of God. He gave His son, and Jesus gave his life, to exonerate us from the penalty of sin. Hallelujah! Sin no longer has power over us, who believe.

THE SONS OF GOD
– DESCENDANTS OF
THE GODLY LINE

God extended his kindness to Adam and Eve by giving them another son. Seth (the good son) was given to them for the death of Abel. Often when God allows something to be taken away, the replacement is a greater blessing.

I remember when my husband was in the United States Air Force, and we were stationed in Denver Colorado. We were members of the Antioch Church of God in Christ under the leadership of Pastor Frank Elijah Johnson. While stationed there a young couple who had relocated, united with the church under the watch care of our pastor. They had recently gotten married and the Lord blessed them to conceive a child.

When the time came for her delivery, the baby was still born. She delivered a beautiful baby girl, and her heart was broken. But God who knows how to comfort, during the process of time, blessed them to conceive again, and deliver twin boys. They were strong and healthy. Although the twins could not replace the child they lost, the joy of having them eased the pain.

While in the Philippine islands in 1985 I had a miscarriage. I told myself "I am going to go through this without any problems"; but I didn't count on the emotional aftermath. When you have life in your body and lose that life it leaves an empty feeling. All of the excitement of one day holding your baby in your arms and watching him/her grow will never be realized. That hurts! My heart goes out to all the ladies who have experienced the loss of a child. May God ever strengthen you.

God has been so gracious to Joseph and me, blessing us to conceive and deliver two healthy children after that miscarriage. God cares for his people; and many times blesses them with double for their trouble.

The King James Version declares that Eve said: "God had appointed me another seed instead of Abel whom Cain slew." (Genesis 4:25 KJV)

Usage of the word "appointed" indicates that Eve may have received a divine communication from God, concerning Seth. God set and placed, this seed for the continuation of mankind. Seth's posterity continued after the flood, when all the other families of the earth were destroyed. Noah was the tenth descendant from Adam through Seth. It was from the line of Seth that the Messiah would come.

"And to Seth was born a son, and he name him Enos: then began men to call upon the name of the Lord." (Genesis 4:26 KJV) Seth's family called on the name of the Lord to express their dependency on him. Giving birth to public prayer and worship, in which Enos was the pioneer.

From that point on, there began to be a distinction between men. "Two completely different family groups developed on earth, the godly and the ungodly."

(Fire Bible commentary Chap. 4:26 pg.42)

And while the world stands there will be a continuance of the same.

"The number of people on earth continued to increase. When these people had daughters, the sons of God (Seth line) saw how beautiful they were. So, they chose the women they wanted. They married them, and the women had their children."

(Genesis 6:1-2 ERV) "The Lord saw how great the wickedness of the human race had become on the earth, and that every inclination of the thoughts of the human heart was only evil all the time. The Lord regretted that he had made human beings on the earth, and his heart was deeply troubled. So the Lord said, I will wipe from the face of the earth the human race I have created." (Genesis.6: 5-7a NIV)

The posterity of Seth was to be the ones to honor God, but there was a breakdown in the linage.

The seed of Seth lusted after the daughters from the seed of Cain. The ungodly line mixing with the godly. Without the power of God working in man, more *ungodliness* will be produced. And that is exactly what happened! Sin and holiness will never mix. When one follows the dictates of their fleshly nature (which is corrupt) the results is sin. Unless a sinner repents and turn in obedience to the living God, he/ she will remain in a disconnected state. The redemptive line of Seth (the sons of God) had not lived up to their full potential. They begin to intermarry with the ungodly family of Cain. Because of these unions wickedness began to increase in the earth.

The increase of sin in the earth was in part due to the error in the redemptive line of the sons of God. It was the lust of the eye, which lured them to sin before God. They had grown so preoccupied with evil that the entire world turned out to be corrupt and filled with violence.

"Don't love the world's ways. Don't love the world's goods. Love of the world squeezes out love for the Father. Practically everything that goes on in the world - wanting your own way, wanting everything for yourself, wanting to appear important - has nothing to do with the Father. It just isolates you from him.

The world and all its wanting, wanting, wanting is on its way out-but whoever does what God wants is set for eternity."(1 John 2:15-17 MSG)

The term world in the New Testament refers to a group of social, economic or political practices that exists apart from God. Mankind, choosing their desires, above the will of God. Being in opposition to God's word, his people and his purpose. "This is how the world has operated since the first humans gave in to Satan's temptation and brought the curse of sin into the earth and upon all creation. This disobedience to God has matriculated down through humanity even into this present time." 1.

"The god of this age (Satan) has blinded the minds of unbelievers, so that they cannot see the light of the gospel that displays the glory of Christ, who is the image of God." (2 Corinthians 4:4 NIV)

"Mankind gave up his authority through defiance of God. Satan gained control and manipulated the endeavors of man with selfishness and immorality." 2.

(Fire Bible Global Study Edition (1&2) "The Christian's Relationship to the World" 1John 2:15-16 pg. 2472)

But one man stood up for righteousness in a time when corruption was in all the earth: The man Noah!

PART TWO

The Man Noah

"Noah was warned by God about things that he could not see. But he had faith and respect for God, so he built a large boat to save his family. With his faith, Noah showed that the world was wrong. And he became one of those who are made right with God through faith." Hebrews 11:7 ERV

NOAH

"But Noah found grace (favor) in the eyes of The Lord. This is the history of the generation of Noah. Noah was a just and righteous man, blameless in his [evil] generation; Noah walked [in habitual fellowship] with God." (Genesis 6:8-9AMP)

Noah's name derived from the Hebrew word (Noach) meaning peace/rest and comfort.

He was the tenth generation beginning with Adam. Noah was of the lineage of Seth, which was called the "royal" line, because Seth believed and followed God.

God's plan far reaches individuals, it extends to and through generations.

When God looks at you, "He sees your ancestors, He sees your children and grandchildren." 1. He is the God of the family.

(Matthew 1:17KJV) says; "So the generations from Abraham to David are fourteen generations; and from David until the carrying away into Babylon are fourteen generations; and from the carrying away into Babylon unto Christ are fourteen generations."

"When God made a covenant with Abraham, He said "In blessing I will bless you, and multiplying I will multiply your descendants as the stars of the heaven and as the sand which is on the seashore; and your descendants shall possess the gate of their enemies. In your seed all the nations of the earth shall be blessed, because you have obeyed My voice. Because of Abraham's obedience to God his descendants also were blessed." 2. (Genesis 22:17-18 KJV) That's what I call blood line blessings.

(https://walkingbyfaith.tv/breaking-generational-curses/ Duane Vander Klok 1,2)

In (Genesis 5:29 AMP) Lamech named his son Noah and said, "This one shall bring us rest and comfort from our work and from the [dreadful] toil of our hands because of the ground which the Lord has cursed." He was the great grandson of Enoch who walked with God and was translated. It was Enoch's undeniable, unshakable faith that enabled him not to experience death.

(Hebrews 11:5-6 MSG) says: "By an act of faith, Enoch skipped death completely. They looked all over and couldn't find him because God had taken him. We know on the basis of reliable testimony that before he was taken, he pleased God. It's impossible to please God apart from faith. And why? Because anyone who approaches God must believe both that he exists and that he cares enough to respond to those who seek him." Enoch was a great example of intimacy with God.

(Bible-truth.org "The Genealogy of the Royal Line from Adam to Noah")

NOAH FOUND FAVOR WITH GOD

"Everyone else in those days lived wickedly, but Noah worshiped, obeyed and depended upon God. He was not influenced by the immorality that surrounded him. In character, he was just and righteous with a deep respect for God and a bold resistance to popular opinion and behavior." (Genesis 6:9 Notes Fire Bible pg.44)

Noah believed what God said concerning the disaster that was to take place in the earth; even though they had never seen rain. He was willing to risk his reputation and trust that God's warning of rain would come to pass.

John Wooden wrote: "Be more concerned with your character than your reputation, because your character is what you really are, while your reputation is merely what others think you are." www.azquotes. com John Wooden Quotes About Character

Noah had impeccable character in his time. He was righteous in the sight of his creator. Righteousness is right standing with God, not human perfection. It is a gift of God's grace – not something you can earn or achieve. The Father simply declares your innocence from the penalty of sin, according to your faith. God extended His grace to Noah, and Noah had faith in God. "Salvation is a result of God's mercy and grace received by faith; and demonstrated by sincerity in obedience to God's word." (Genesis 6:9 notes Fire Bible pg. 44)

"Our righteousness are as filthy rags." (Isaiah 64:6 KJV) We cannot live good enough to be acceptable to a holy and righteous God. None of us can be saved by moral perfection. So as believers we don't stand before God in our righteousness, but in the righteousness of God through Jesus Christ. Humanity must take on the righteousness of God. (Romans 10: 9-10 Amp) states: "if you acknowledge and confess with your mouth that Jesus is Lord [recognizing His power, authority, and majesty as God], and believe in your heart that God raised Him from the dead, you will be saved. For with the heart a person believes [in Christ as Savior] resulting in his justification [that is, being made righteous—being freed of the guilt of sin and made acceptable to God]; and with the mouth he acknowledges and confesses [his faith openly], resulting in and confirming [his] salvation.

The scripture states: "and if He did not spare the ancient world, but protected Noah, a preacher of righteousness, with seven others, when He brought [the judgment of] a flood upon the world of the ungodly; and if He condemned the cities of Sodom and Gomorrah to destruction by reducing them to ashes, having made them an example to those who would live ungodly lives thereafter; and if He rescued righteous Lot, who was tormented by the immoral conduct of unprincipled and ungodly men, then [in light of the fact that all this is true, be sure that] the Lord knows how to rescue the godly from trial, and how to keep the unrighteous under punishment until the day of judgment," (2 Peter 2:5-7,9 AMP)

THE POWER OF ONE

The dictionary defines this statement as the capacity of a single person to direct or influence the behavior of others, or the course of events. One man or one woman with the power of God operating in their life, can change the direction of events in the world. The power of one, can influence others and history for the betterment of humanity. People like Mohandas Gandhi, Rosa Parks and Martin Luther King have made a great difference in this world. (www.biographyonline. net>events>changed-world-better)

Noah in his time was such a man.

God anointed Noah to warn mankind of the coming judgment. He enabled him to persevere and accomplish the task that was set before him. "By faith [with confidence in God and His word] Noah, being warned by God about events not yet seen, in reverence prepared an ark for the salvation of his family. By this [act of obedience] he condemned the world and became and heir of the righteousness which comes by faith." (Hebrews 11:7 AMP) Just as Noah had to make a choice in his day, we have to make a choice in our day. "Choose ye this day whom you will serve" Joshua said to the children of Israel in (Joshua 24:15 KJV) "whether the gods which your fathers served that were on the other side of the flood, or the gods of the Amorites, in whose land ye dwell: but as for me and my house, we will serve the Lord." There will always be a war between good and evil, right and wrong, godliness and selfishness, until God's eternal peace reigns on the earth. Who will you choose? What will be your God?

Years ago, when my children were adolescents, they went into a local department store. Three of them were together, when they were confronted with the decision of right or wrong. While in the store they were tempted to go against what they were taught. Two decided to take something that didn't belong to them. They probably thought it was a foolproof plan. The two older ones chose to take some clothing items and the youngest of the three refused. I can see her telling them (with a little sassiness) "y'all gonna get in trouble." As they were leaving the store the security guard stopped them and took them in the office. We were called, and they had to face the penalty for their crime by their father. Some lessons learned early in life saves one from greater consequences in the future. They learned that there are consequences for wrongdoing. Sooner or later everyone will be confronted with that same decision. The wrong decision is going to eventually cause pain.

Noah exemplified moral and mental strength. He didn't cower in the midst of fear, danger and difficulty. He was obedient to every command that was given to him! God expects the same from you and me.

He waited patiently after the rain had abated from the earth, until God told him to go forward. God's timing should be our timing! Quick moves may bring pitfalls and danger. Delays may cause doors of opportunity to be closed. Trust God!

"And Noah built an altar unto the Lord; and took of every clean beast, and of every clean fowl, and offered burnt offerings on the altar. And the Lord smelled a sweet savor; and the Lord said in his heart, I will not again curse the ground any more for man's sake; for the imagination of man's heart is evil from his youth; neither will I again smite any more everything living, as I have done." (Genesis 8:20-21 KJV)

Noah building an altar illustrated his relationship to God. Before this act in history, Noah had done nothing without specific instructions from God. God called him to prepare the Ark, told him what animals to bring into the Ark, when to go in and when to come out. These instructions were obeyed to the letter. But building an altar and offering sacrifices (which was already established as religious worship) he needed no command. Being thankful for God's mercy, was his motivation. And the worship of his heart was a pleasing aroma to his heavenly father.

FAITH

Belief and complete trust in and loyalty to God. (Merriam-Webster)

Faith led Noah to listen when God warned him about the things in the future that he could not see. He obeyed God and built a ship to save his family. Through faith Noah condemned the world and received God's approval that comes through faith." (Heb.11:7 GW)

"Without faith no one can please God. Whoever comes to God must believe that he is real and that he rewards those who sincerely try to find him." (Heb. 11:6 ERV) "Believing in the Biblical sense is not just a mental exercise; it is an active faith that yields the leadership of one's life to Christ." (Notes: fire Bible John 1:12 pg. 1906)

Real faith is a strong conviction and trust in God, and the tenacity to obey His command despite difficulties. It pushes one into a deeper and profound love relationship with Christ.

Faith is about hearing the voice of God inwardly, through the written word or through the preached word. It's about receiving what the Lord has spoken as truth. This causes one to realize that we need the Lord's intervention in every aspect of our lives.

March 1984 was my first experience on an airplane. It was a sixteen-hour flight to the Philippine islands. Petrified, my stomach felt like it was tied in knots and the turbulence added to my anxiety. I was tied to this experience with no escape in sight. The anticipation of getting out of the air, off that plane and my feet on God's great earth consumed my thoughts. My children were having a great time; they were excited. My son Anthony wanted me to look out of the window, I refused, with an anxious no. It was not until the Holy Spirit reminded me that the anxiety I was feeling was not of God. At that point I began to fight in faith and continued the fight until we landed. We flew from Los Angeles, California to Seattle, Washington and from Seattle to Anchorage, Alaska, from Alaska to Okinawa, Japan and from Okinawa to Angeles City, Philippines landing on Clark Air Force Base. Thirty minutes into the flight from Japan to the Philippines; the pilot put on the fasten seat belt light and announced we were about to land. We were previously told this would be a two-hour flight. Whether it was an instrument malfunction or pilot inexperience it left me feeling very uncomfortable. When he discovered we were not as close as anticipated, the light was turned off, and we continued toward our destination. We started the descent to the Philippines. As we got closer the plane began to rapidly drop in altitude, several times. Like being on the highest point of a roller coaster and the cars plummet downward at an accelerated speed. It Felt like my stomach was in my throat, my eyes were shut tight, and my emotions were anticipating the end. At this point in the flight I knew I needed the Lord's intervention and began to call on the name of Jesus! Thank God we had a safe landing. When I stepped off the plane, it was like stepping into an oven. This was the hottest place I had ever encountered. I failed to mention earlier, I was six months pregnant. This was a time of new experiences. I realize my faith was being tested to prepare me for future challenges. Readers help me say: *A Dispensation for a New Level of Trust*

If man knew everything and understood all things there would be no need to trust in God for anything.

FAITH ALIVE AND ACTIVE!

Martin Luther said: "Faith is God's work in us that changes us and gives us new birth from God. (Taken from John 1:13 KJV)

It kills the Adamic nature and makes us different people. It changes our hearts, our spirits, and our thoughts. It is a living, creative, active and powerful thing.

Faith gives confidence and knowledge of God's grace which makes you happy, joyful and bold in your relationship to God and all creation.

One will freely, willingly and joyfully do good to everyone. Suffering all kinds of things, with a continual love and praise for God who has shown you such grace. Ask God to work faith in you, or you will remain forever without faith, no matter what you wish, say or can do." (Martin Luther's Definition of Faith: Translated by Rev. Robert E. Smith - "An Introduction to St. Paul's letter to the Romans)"

A congregational song comes to mind: It says, "Get in the Word and stay there, stay til Jesus comes." (https://youtu.be/FUJHwVVbU5Y TC "Get In The Word & Stay There; Be Ready When Jesus Comes" By TC & The Smith Brothers)

"So then faith cometh by hearing, and hearing by the word of God."

(Romans 10:17 KJV)

One must be active in the study of God's word, meditating on it and praying for an understanding from God.

"I have been crucified with Christ and I no longer live, but Christ lives in me. The life I now live in the body, I live by faith in the Son of God, who loved me and gave himself for me." (Gal. 2:20 NIV) The yielding of one's self to God, by faith is a Sweet Aroma to The Lord!

VICTORY OVER FEAR

Fear, an unpleasant emotion caused by the belief that someone or something is dangerous, likely to cause pain, or a threat. Fear is a spirit.

"For God hath not given us the spirit of fear, but of power, and of love, and of a sound mind." (2 Timothy 1:7 KJV)

Fear is a crippling, stifling spirit that will latch on to your thoughts; if you let it remain active. It will stop one from moving forward in the things of God and hinder your destiny. Through Christ, we have power to overcome fear and every barrier the enemy puts in our way. Christ gives us the victory!

The need for victory implies a struggle. Christian's experience warfare against sin, hardships and adversities in our everyday lives. But through faith in Jesus We Win! "For everyone who has been born of God overcomes the world. And this is the victory that has overcome the world - our faith. Who is it that overcomes the world except the one who believes that Jesus is the Son of God?" (1 John 5:4-5 ASV) Paul encourages his son in the gospel in (1Timothy 6:12 KJV) "Fight the good fight of faith [in the conflict with evil]; take hold of the eternal life, to which you were called, and [for which] you made the good confession [of faith] in the presence of many witnesses."

Noah's faith honored God. He exhibited courage in a chaotic time. God is calling for believer today to have courage, stand up for righteousness and trust Him in this world's present darkness.

Situations will arise that will not be easy, but remember God is with you and the Holy Spirit will help you. Trust God's love, his provisions and his protection. And He will manifest your victory.

PART THREE

Honor

MAN'S GREATEST HONOR AND PRIVILEGE
IS TO DO THE WILL OF GOD
Zac Poonen

"God is greatly to be feared in the assembly of the saints, and to be had in reverence of all them that are about him. O Lord God of hosts, who is a strong Lord like unto thee? or to thy faithfulness round about thee?" Psalm 89 7-8 KJV

HONOR

"Then Noah built an altar to honor the Lord. Noah took some of all the clean birds and some of all the clean animals and burned them on the altar as a gift to God." (Gen. 8:20 ERV)

Honor God: give Him respect for His ability, His qualities and for what He has done. It is to offer the Lord the adoration and worship that is due Him.

At this time in history Noah was six hundred and one years old. He had been in the ark one year and ten days, when God spoke to him and told him to come out of the ark. Noah was to bring out his family, all the animals, the crawling things, the birds and whatever moves on the land. Noah built an altar to honor Yahweh (the God of Israel). He took special care in what kind of sacrifices he offered. Ceremonially clean animals and birds were presented as burnt offering to God. The Hebrew word for burnt offering means to go up in smoke. As the smoke from the sacrifice ascended, it was "a soothing aroma to the Lord." Noah worshipped and respected God, and it was evident by his actions.

God spoke to Noah in a time when wickedness was running rampant in the earth. Men were doing everything imaginable. God said it was going to rain and to build an ark. He cried out to the people, preaching to them concerning the coming flood and the need to repent. But they mocked him and brought upon themselves judgement. God "spared not the old world, but saved Noah the eighth person, a preacher of righteousness, bringing in the flood upon the world of the ungodly;" (2 Peter 2:5 KJV)

All the animals were brought in; the creeping things, the birds and all that God had instructed him, and God shut the door. It rained for forty days and forty nights. And water stayed on the earth for five months. Considering all that took place in Noah's life he was obedient to God. God took care of him, his family, and every living thing in the ark. I can imagine how relieved they must have been to finally see dry ground. Their lives were spared when the whole world had been destroyed. Thank God for His Mercy!

What a great privilege it is to show honor to the almighty God. Solomon in the beginning of his reign demonstrated such honor. The Lord granted him wealth along with wisdom and knowledge. In the first chapter of second Chronicles Solomon and the congregation sought the Lord on the brazen altar; on it he offered a thousand burnt offerings. That same night God appeared to Solomon and said, ask for whatever you want. Solomon asked the Lord for wisdom and knowledge to judge His people. Because of Solomon's heart for God's people, he was granted wisdom, knowledge, riches and honor. God bestowed upon him such honor that none had before him nor will ever have after him. (2 Chronicles 1:5-12 KJV)

In the second chapter of second Chronicles, Solomon was determined to build a house for the name of the Lord and for his kingdom. He said in the fifth verse; "the house which I build is great: for great is our God above all gods." (2 Chronicles 2:5 KJV)

He took every precaution to make sure that God's house was superb. The materials used were the best and the men hired were expert in their craft. It was evident that Solomon honored God; his actions exhibited his heart.

In the fifth chapter of Second Chronicles Solomon had finished the Lords house. He brought in all the things that David; his father had dedicated for the house of God. The elders, the tribal heads, and the chief of the fathers of the children of Israel assembled to Jerusalem to bring up the ark of the covenant of the Lord out of the city of David, which is Zion. (2 Chronicles 5:2 KJV)

The priest brought in the ark of the covenant of the Lord and placed it in the Holy of Holies. The Levites sang, and one hundred twenty priests blew the trumpets as to make one sound in praising the Lord. They sang: "The Lord is good, His mercy endureth forever." (2 Chron. 5:13KJV) And the almighty God honored them by filling the house with his presence. The priests could not continue to serve because of the cloud (the glory of the Lord had filled the Temple.(2 Chronicles 5:7, 12-14 KJV)

If one demonstrates love for God, by striving to do everything for Him in excellence; they will be honored by God. What greater honor is there, above being in his presence, witnessing His Holiness, and feeling his love surrounding you? There is none!

"In His presence is the fullness of joy; In His right hand there are pleasures forevermore." (Ps. 16:11 AMP)

"Now the Lord is that Spirit, and where the Spirit of the Lord is, there is liberty [emancipation from bondage, true freedom]." (2 Cor. 3:17 AMP)

Even when God makes your name great; the best place, the safest place, the most desirable place to be is close to Him.

In November 1995, our last duty station, in the Air force was San Antonio Texas. We became members of the Anderson Temple COGIC. After being members there for a while our pastor, Geoffrey Stirrup felt comfortable in giving us a key. I was impressed by the Holy Spirit to take Thursdays to go up to the church and pray. This was a wonderful time of peace in the presence of the Lord. I talked to Him and I would hear his voice speak to me. It was not an audible voice but one inwardly. At times I would sing to the Lord and feel his presence so strongly, until tears would roll down my face. My arms would raise, my voice would elevate, and a shout of HALLELUJAH followed! Sometimes I was so joyful that I would even dance before the Lord, all by myself. What a wonderful love relationship was developed with me and my savior.

Moses in the book of Exodus, had an awesome privilege in the presence of God. In the time spent on Mount Sinai, he communed with the almighty. He didn't need food or drink; the presence of the Lord was food and drink enough. Mary, the sister of Martha: in Luke chapter ten, realized that being in Jesus presence was the most desirable place. She chose to set at His feet and hear wisdom from his lips, while Martha was busy with serving. (Luke 10:38-40 KJV)

I'm reminded of a song and the lyrics says: "In Your presence is where I long to be, it's the place where I can be closest to thee, So I worship you the more for it opens up a door into your presence, is where I long to be, your presence is where I long to be."(In Your Presence Pt.1 Bishop Paul S. Morton Sr. & Full Gospel Baptist Church Fellowship Women's Mass Choir Daughters of the Promise provided by YouTube)

"O come, let us worship and bow down: let us kneel before the Lord our maker. For he is our God; and we are the people of his pasture, and sheep of his hand." (Psalm 95:6-7 KJV) His presence is truly the place of honor!

God promises in the book of James to come close to the believer who purifies his heart and seeks a deep relationship with Him. The one who spends time in prayer and in God's Word can experience the presence of the Holy Spirit. If we "humble ourselves [with an attitude of repentance and insignificance] in the presence of the Lord, He will exalt you [He will lift you up, He will give you purpose]." (James 4:10AMP)

PRAISE

Praise is ones expression of respect and gratitude toward God. It is to worship, glorify, honor, exalt, and adore Him.

God the Creator

"In the beginning God (Elohim) created [by forming from nothing] the heavens and the earth." (Genesis 1:1 AMP) God in his infinite wisdom and power created this earth with all of its beauty, for humankind. The detail Father God put in this world is more than magnificent. God took care in everything he made, so that man could live and thrive, in his habitation. Vegetation and fruit had seeds in them to reproduce. He created animals, birds, fish and insects of various kinds, all with purpose and capability to multiply. Our heavenly Father made seasons, gave us the sun for light in the day and stars and the moon for light at night. After preparing a suitable place for him to live, God made man and called him Adam. He took a rib from his side to make a companion/helper, whom Adam called woman and later named her Eve.

"The earth is the Lord's, and the fulness thereof; the world, and they that dwell therein. For He hath founded it upon the seas, and established it upon the floods." (Psalm 24:1-2 KJV)

"The heavens declare the glory of God and the firmament sheweth his handywork (Psalm 19:1 KJV)

"By faith we understand that the universe was created by the word of God, so that what is seen was not made out of things that are visible." (Hebrews 11:3 ESV)

"When I look at the heavens, the work of your fingers, the moon and the stars, which you set in place, what is man that you are mindful of him, and the son of man that you care for him?" (Psalm 8:3-4 ESV)

"He (Jesus/son of man) is the radiance of the glory of God and the exact imprint of his nature, and he upholds the universe by the word of his power. After making purification for sins, he sat down at the right hand of the Majesty on high." (Hebrews 1:3 ESV)

How can anyone believe that all of the world's beauty, detail and variety came from the process of Nucleosynthesis. "This theory is the process that creates new atomic nuclei from pre-existing nucleons (protons and neutrons) and nuclei. According to current theories, the first nuclei were formed a few minutes after the Big Bang; through nuclear reactions in a process called Big Bang nucleosynthesis. (Primordial – Wikipedia https://en.m.wikipedia.org)

The Psalmist gives the credit for making the complexity of man to God and so do I.

"Then God said, "Let us make man in our image, after our likeness, And let them have dominion over the fish of the sea and over the birds of the heavens and over every creeping thing that creeps on the earth." (Genesis 1:26 ESV)

The Psalmist said: "Oh yes you shaped me first inside, then out; you formed me in my mother's womb. I thank you, High God-you're breathtaking! Body and soul, I am marvelously made! I worship in adoration-what a creation! You know me inside and out, you know every bone in my body; you know exactly how I was made, bit by bit, how I was sculpted from nothing into something. Like an open book, you watched me grow from conception to birth; all the stages of my life were spread out before you, the days of my life all prepared before I'd even lived one day." (Psalms 139:13-16 MSG)

"Human life begins at fertilization (conception): a sperm cell connecting to an egg (oocyte) to produce a new human organism. This individual is called a zygote at the one-cell stage of development, an embryo through the first eight weeks, and a fetus from eight weeks until birth. Each of us was once a zygote, embryo, and fetus, just as we were once infants, toddlers, and adolescents. All of these terms refer to stages in the life of a member of the species Homo sapiens (scientific name for human beings)." (https://www.mccl.org>prenataldeve.)

How marvelous is God's handiwork!

"A developed human being has eleven (11) systems that make up his/her body: Integumentary system, skeletal system, muscular system, nervous system, endocrine system, circulatory system, lymphatic system, respiratory system, digestive system, urinary/excretory system and the reproductive systems." (http://study.com>...College Biology: What is an Organ System?- Definition & Pictures- Biology)

"And God blessed them [granted them certain authority] and said to them, "Be fruitful, multiply, and fill the earth, and subjugate it [putting it under your power]; and rule over (dominate) the fish of the sea, the birds of the air, and every living thing that moves upon the earth." (Genesis 1: 28 AMP)

Our existence in this earth realm is to have fellowship with the Father, so he made us body, soul and spirit. Our body was made to live in the earth; "It's the most visible part of our being." The soul is not seen, but it is where one finds emotions, reasoning, decision making, joy and sadness. The soul makes up our personality. I believe the soul helps human beings have fellowship with each other. "The spirit is the deepest and most hidden part of our being. It connects us to the spirit realm," which enables man to fellowship with God.

(The Three Parts of Man blog.biblesforamerica.org)

"Now may the God of peace Himself sanctify you through and through [that is, separate you from profane and vulgar things, make you pure and whole and undamaged-consecrated to Him-set apart for His purpose]; and may your spirit and soul and body be kept complete and [be found] blameless at the coming of our Lord Jesus Christ." (1Thessalonians 5:23 AMP)

God deserves all the praise! "For in Him we live and move and exist [that is, in Him we actually have our being]." (Acts 17:28 AMP) In light of the fact God made us it's right for us to praise Him." So let us "rejoice in the Lord, you righteous ones; Praise is becoming and appropriate for those who are upright [in heart-those with moral integrity and godly character]." (Psalm 33:1 AMP)

Everything that has life ought to praise the Lord. "Let every living, breathing creature praise God! Hallelujah!" (Psalm 150:6 MSG)

When one has a true knowledge of who God is and who we are, praising God is a common thing. We joyfully honor Him with the fruit of our lips, singing praises to His name. It is an outward expression of an inward revelation.

"Rejoice in the Lord, O ye righteous: for praise is comely for the upright."

(Psalm 33:1 KJV)

"Praise ye the Lord: for it is good to sing praises unto our God; for it is pleasant; and praise is comely." (Psalm 147:1 KJV)

We understand that "it is he that has made us and not we ourselves."

(Psalm 100:3 KJV) Our very being was created by the almighty God.

"Give praise to the Lord, proclaim his name; make known among the nations what he has done." (Psalm 105:1 NIV)

Apostle Paul asked the saints at Ephesus, to pray for him, that whenever he would speak, words would be given him so that without fear he would make known the mystery of the gospel. Declaring to be an ambassador of the gospel in chains. (Ephesians 6:19-20 NIV)

Shouldn't we all be ambassadors for Christ?

Honor God with praise and He will honor you with power!

King Jehoshaphat and Judah were faced with enemies from Ammon, Moab and Mount Seir, who came up against them to battle. Judah's faith in their God, was demonstrated through praying and singing praises to Him. Because of their faith God set ambushes against their enemies. (2 Chronicles 20:1-22 NIV)

In July 1978 when my mother transitioned this life, I received the baptism of the Holy Ghost. My husband and I came to church that night, set in the service and heard the word of God. Our pastor (Elder Frank Johnson) called for those who desired prayer to come to the altar. I proceeded to go to the altar and begin to praise God for saving my mother. The Spirit of the Lord spoke to me and said release yourself; in my limited understanding I felt the Lord was saying don't try to hold yourself up. So I fell to the floor. At that time I felt something moving in my belly. The Lord purged me, and I spoke in an unknown tongue. God empowered me with his spirit.

HUMILITY

Merriam-Webster defines humility as: "freedom from pride or arrogance: the quality or state of being humble.

"When pride comes [boiling up with an arrogant attitude of self-importance], then comes dishonor and shame, But with the humble [the teachable who have been chiseled by trial and who have learned to walk humbly with God] there is wisdom and soundness of mind." (Proverbs 11:2 AMP)

Humility before The Lord shows that one honors Him. Jesus Christ was the perfect example of humility.

The Apostle Paul encouraged the Philippian Christians to grow in humility, reminding them of the lowliness of Jesus. He expressed to them that: Jesus was like God in every way, but he did not use that to His advantage. Leaving his place with God, He put on human flesh and assumed the role of a servant. Christ humbled Himself and was obedient to God, even unto the death on the cross. So, God highly exalted Him and gave him the name above all names. (Phil. 2:6-9 ERV) Considering what we just read; scripture admonishes us to give ourselves to God. "So, submit to [the authority of] God. Resist the devil [stand firm against him] and he will flee from you. Come close to God [with a contrite heart] and He will come close to you. Wash your hands, you sinners; and purify your [unfaithful] hearts, you double-minded [people]. Be miserable and grieve and weep [over your sin]. Let your [foolish] laughter be turned to mourning and your [reckless] joy to gloom. Humble yourselves [with an attitude of repentance and insignificance] in the presence of the Lord, and He will exalt you [He will lift you up, He will give you purpose]." (James 4:7-10 AMP) The Message bible says: "The fun and games are over. Get serious, really serious. Get down on your knees before the Master; it's the only way you'll get on your feet." (James 4:10b MSG) If one desires to know God, a humble heart is the key. It must be God's will, as specified in His word, and not ours.

In the book of 2 Kings the twenty-second chapter King Josiah, who was a good king, sent his scribe to the high priest Hilkiah to count money given for the repair of the house of God. Hilkiah had found the Book of the Law in the house of the Lord, and gave it to Shaphan the scribe, and he read it. The scribe read the book to the king, and when Josiah heard the words in the book, he tore his clothes as a sign of his sadness. He then told the high priest, the scribe, and servants to enquire of the Lord what should they do, for he knew that The Lord was very angry. Judah's ancestors didn't listen and obey the words of the book. So the priest, scribe, and the others went to Huldah the prophetess. The Lord gave Huldah a message for King Josiah. The troubles that were spoken of in the book of The Law would happen, because the people of Judah had forsaken God and burned incense to other gods. King Josiah's heart was tender and penitent, he humbled himself and wept before the Lord, and was granted mercy. He and the people that lived in Judah during his reign would not see the destruction that was to come. (2 Kings 22:1-20 KJV)

A person who humbles himself before God and have faith to obey His Word is a successful person.

A writer once penned this colorful truth to success, and it blessed me. He said: "The road to success is not straight. There is a curb called

Failure, a loop called Confusion; speed bumps called Friends; red lights called Enemies; caution lights called Family; and flats called Jobs. But, if you have a spare called Determination; an engine called Perseverance; insurance called Faith, and a driver called Jesus, you will make it to a place called Success!" (Ibrahim: published 8-13-2005 www.arabnews.com)

God gave Joshua a formula for success: "Always remember what is written in that book of law. Speak about that book and study it day and night. Then you can be sure to obey what is written there. If you do this, you will be wise and successful in everything you do." (Joshua 1:8 ERV)

True humility means humbling one-self before men!

We cannot treat each other badly and think we are honoring God. (Philippians 2:3-4 NIV) says: "Do nothing out of selfish ambition or vain conceit. Rather, in humility value others above yourselves, not looking to your own interest but each of you to the interest of the others." (Ephesians 4:2 NIV) "Be completely humble and gentle; be patient, bearing with one another in love."

(Matthew 5:23-24 AMP) says, "So if you are presenting your offering at the altar, and while there you remember that your brother has something [such as a grievance or legitimate complaint] against you, leave your offering there at the altar and go. First make peace with your brother, and then come and present your offering."

One definition of reconciliation is to restore friendly relations. Do we believe that God is pleased with our praise or prayer, when we know we have caused an offense to another believer? Strive to restore unity. One must go to the offended party and try to reconcile. The Bible is right!

Years ago in a Bible study a question was asked, and I responded. One of the young ladies that was present in that study started acting evasive towards me. Whenever I would come near her, she would walk away.

After this avoidance continued for a while, I begin to search myself. I tried to figure out what I could have said or done to make her act in such away. I didn't recall doing anything that would cause a rift in our friendship. We were members of the same church. I decided with the prompting of the Holy Spirit to go to her. When I confronted her, she didn't want to talk about what was bothering her, so I apologized for whatever I did to make her angry. She told me that I was talking about her when we were in Bible study. Puzzled I asked her what I said, she told me. Apologizing again I tried to assure her that I wasn't thinking of her when I answered neither did, I know her business. So she walked away seemly not convinced. As believers we must do our part to reconcile even if it's not received. Pray for the person who was offended.

"Do not offend Jews or Greeks or even the church of God [but live to honor Him]; just as I please everyone in all things [as much as possible adapting myself to the interests of others], not seeking my own benefit but that of the many, so that they [will be open to the message of salvation and] may be saved." (1 Corinthians 10:32-33 AMP)

Below, is a compilation of quotes for your consideration!

Quotes that Remind us of the Awesome Power of Humility:

1. "Never look down on anybody unless you're helping them up." *Jesse Jackson*
2. "Pride makes us artificial, and humility makes us real." *Thomas Merton*
3. "The greatest friend of truth is time, her greatest enemy is prejudice, and her constant companion is humility." *Charles Caleb Colton*
4. "Pride must die in you or nothing of heaven can live in you." *Andrew Murray,* (Humility http//www.inc.com.dave-kerpen)

James E. Faust Quotes American - Clergyman (1920 – 2007)

1. A grateful heart is the beginning of greatness, expressed in humility.
2. Good parents put off many of their own needs and desires in favor of the needs of their children. Such sacrifice develops noble character.
3. We must take the bitter with the sweet. God has a purpose in difficulties confronted.
4. Waiting for people to repent before forgiving them, causes one to lose peace and happiness.
5. Femininity is God's adornment. Demonstrated in capacity to love, in spirituality, sensitivity, creativity, graciousness, gentleness, dignity, and quiet strength.
6. Honesty is telling the truth, speaking truth, living the truth, and loving in truth.
7. One has to live with the consequences of our choices. (*www.brainyquotes.com*> authors >james-e-faust-quotes)

350 Humility Quotes That Will Inspire you to be Humble.

1. "A great man is always willing to be little." *Ralph Waldo Emerson*
2. "Humility will open more doors than arrogance ever will." *Zig Ziglar*
3. "True knowledge exists in knowing that you know nothing." *Socrates*
4. "Mastery begins with humility." *Robin Sharma*
5. "Every person that you meet knows something you don't, learn from them."
   H. Jackson Brown Jr. (WisdomQuotes.com>humility.quotes)

"Do not be overcome by evil, but overcome evil with good." (Romans 12:21 NIV)

SUBSTANCE

One definition of substance is: material possessions (Merriam-Webster)

"Don't trust in your wisdom, but fear and respect the Lord and stay away from evil.

If you do this it will be like a refreshing drink and medicine for your body.

Honor the Lord with your wealth and the first part of your harvest.

Then your barns will be full of grain, and your barrels will be overflowing with wine." (Proverbs 3:7-10 ERV)

"Give, and it shall be given unto you; good measure, pressed down, and shaken together, and running over, shall men give into your bosom. For with the same measure that ye mete withal it shall be measured to you again." (Luke 6:38 KJV)

One honors the Lord by giving back to him, in service to others. God's desire is that we would be a blessing to each other with time and substance. Purposefully allowing ministry to flourish to lost humanity. In so doing we receive a satisfactory and meaningful life.

Lynette Johnson

MONEY IS JUST A TOOL!

My husband and I got saved on Mother's Day 1978 at Antioch Church of God in Christ in Denver Colorado. He came from a household that was living for the Lord, so he knew about giving tithes and offerings. We begin given the Lord the first fruit of our increase. The Lord was true to his word, by supplying all of our needs. Joseph was in the United States Air Force and had to go on a remote tour to Korea in October 1979; we had three children at the time. Our youngest son was five months old and it was the first time we had been separated for any length of time. I applied for food stamps and were able to receive them. I felt impressed in my spirit to give ten percent of the stamps to someone (who was in need) in groceries. My friend and I would go grocery shopping and bless someone, without their knowledge. One of the mother at the church who we blessed got up one Sunday morning during testimony service and said, "somebody put a big box of food on my doorstep, who did it"! She told about what was in the box, and my friend and I was trying hard not to laugh. Oh what joy one receives in their spirit, when blessing someone else. That kind of joy is priceless. The Lord extends a two-fold blessing: to the giver and receiver. It is, more blessed to give than to receive.

Because my husband and I learned the principles of tithing and giving, there has been numerous times the Lord has proven his word to be true in our lives. The Holy Spirit would touch the hearts of people, to give to our family. When I gave birth to my first daughter; our fifth child. One young lady at the church saved her baby girl clothes for about five years or more and gave them to us. They were beautiful: dresses with lace socks and shoes to match, sun dresses, baby rompers, colorful socks and sleepers, all in mint condition, and various sizes. We didn't have to buy any clothing items for our daughter for two years. If one follows God's principle of tithing and giving, the promise will follow.

"Bring the full tithe into the storehouse, that there may be food in my house. And thereby put me to the test, says the Lord of hosts, if I will not open the windows of heaven for you and pour down for you a blessing until there is no more need." (Malachi 3:10 ESV)

Tithes in the Hebrew means: a tenth part.

In God's law the Israelites were required to give one-tenth of their produce, livestock and income. This showed that they knew their blessings came from God. The tithes were the first and best portion of their goods, not the leftovers. God's purpose was the highest priority in life.

Tithes were used for the expense of their place of worship, ceremonial services and support of the priest and Levites.

God holds his people responsible for right management of the resources He has given them. In the parable of the talents in the book of (Matthew 25:15-30 NIV); Jesus's general point to the believer is: "Reward in heaven will be in proportion to his or her commitment to God and faithfulness to use what He has given – regardless of whether it seems like a little or a lot." (Fire Bible note Matt. 25:29 pg.1750)

Those who feel that tithes are just an Old Testament practice that does not apply to us today may be ignoring the bigger picture. God has called us to be givers, submitting our lives to God joyfully. And tithing and giving are meant to bring joy and blessings. There is a lot of controversy about giving ten percent of one's income and I don't pretend to know all the answers. I do know that my husband, myself, my children, and people I know have been blessed by giving tithes unto the Lord. My husband and I have been impressed to give more than ten percent. The greater the sacrifice, the greater the blessing. These are the scriptures in the New Testament that mention tithing: (Matthew 23:23 KJV; Luke 11:42 KJV; 18:12 KJV; Hebrews 7:5-10 KJV).

Tithing is an act of faith! It is easy to give when you have an abundance, but one must believe God to give a designated amount when times are difficult. One's faith is tried when finances are tight. Perhaps God wants to see how much we really love and honor Him, by how we give to others. Our heart's desire should be to give back to the one who has given us so much. Trusting in the Lord to take care of us in difficult times. If one honors God in giving, they can expect a greater return.

"Give to others, and you will receive. You will be given much. It will be poured into your hands – more than you can hold. You will be given so much that it will spill into your lap. The way you give to others is the way God will give to you" (Luke 6:38 ERV)

In the book of Hebrews the seventh chapter verses one through ten; Abraham gave tithes to Melchizedek (whose name signifies righteous king). Melchizedek parallels Jesus Christ who is the Lord of our righteousness. He was the king of Salem (king of peace), and so is Jesus. Christ speaks of peace, creates peace, and is our peacemaker. Melchizedek was the priest of the Most High God, and so is the Lord Jesus. He was without genealogy to be a suitable type of Christ. He met Abraham returning from battle and gave him and his servants' bread and wine to refresh them. In return Abraham gave him a tenth of all the spoil. Matthew Henry said: "Abraham did this as an expression of gratitude for what Melchizedek had done for him. And thus are we obliged to make all possible returns of love and gratitude to the Lord Jesus for all the rich and royal favors' we receive from him." (Matthew Henry's Commentary)

Believers are to share our substance with the messengers of the gospel.

"Don't you know that those who serve in the temple get their food from the temple, and that those who serve at the altar share in what is offered on the altar? In the same way, the Lord has commanded that those who preach the gospel should receive their living from the gospel." (1 Corinthians 9:13 NIV)

In Numbers the eighteenth chapter verses eight thru ten; the Lord spoke to Aaron (the priest), whom he put in charge of the offerings. God relayed to him that part of the offerings given was for himself and his children. God placed in motion, support for the priest and Levites through the offerings the people would give. This principle is still in effect today. God designed for the ones who carry the burden of the gospel to receive the blessings of the gospel. (Numbers 18:8 ERV)

Paul said in (1Corinthians 9:11 AMP) "If we have sown [the good seed of] spiritual things in you, is it too much if we reap material things from you?"

There is a definite relationship between Christians today and God's law.

Jesus said that He didn't come to destroy the law but to fulfill the law. (Matt. 5:17-18). Jesus came to give the full meaning of the law of Moses and the prophets. God desirers that the principles of the law would be in man's heart and walked out in their daily lives.

In addition to tithes the Israelites were required to bring various offerings to the Lord, mostly in the form of sacrifices. (Lev. 1-7 NIV) They could also bring a freewill offering; giving God whatever extra they wanted to give.

The Reason Determines the Results!

(2 Corinthians 9:6-8 ESV) "The point is this: whoever sows sparingly will also reap sparingly, and whoever sows bountifully will also reap bountifully. Each one must give as he has decided in his heart, not reluctantly or under compulsion, for God loves a cheerful giver. And God is able to make all grace abound to you, so that having all sufficiency in all things at all times, you may abound in every good work." It is important to have knowledge of why we give and the right attitude when we give.

When we are giving acts of kindness it shouldn't be done for recognition.

God gives to us and causes increase in our lives, not only naturally but also spiritually. He causes believers to be rich in every way, so that we can always freely give to others. And our giving will cause people to give thanks to God. Your service of giving is proof of faith. People will praise God for you giving to them and for following the Good News of Jesus Christ. In return prayers will be offered up for you. We thank God for the wonderful gift (a giving spirit), and great grace he has given to believers. (2 Corinthians 9:10-15 NIV)

In 1985 the Lord impressed upon my husband to give God more. Each year we sowed 1% more into our tithes. The first year we gave eleven percent tithes, the following year we gave twelve percent tithes until we were up to giving twenty percent tithes. The Lord has blessed us, and as you continue to read you will discover some of the blessings bestowed upon us by the Father.

Alert! Greed and fear will try to be your guide.

God told Moses that He would cause food to fall from the sky. He instructed the children of Israel, after delivering them from Egypt, not to gather more Manna than a day's worth except on the weekend. They were told not to keep it overnight but some disobeyed and found worms in the Manna the next day. (Exodus 16:4-5; 17-22 KJV) Lesson to learn: God is our source, obey Him and don't be afraid. He will supply our needs.

"But those who [are not financially ethical and] crave to get rich [with a compulsive, greedy longing for wealth] fall into temptation and a trap and into many foolish and harmful desires that plunge people into ruin and destruction [leading to personal misery]." (1 Timothy 6:9 AMP)

"Do not store up for yourselves [material] treasures on earth, where moths and rust destroy, and where thieves break in and steal. But store up for yourselves treasures in heaven, where moths nor rust do not destroy, and where thieves do not break in and steal, for where your treasure is, there your heart [your wishes, your desires; that on which your life centers] will be also." (Matthew 6:19-20 AMP)

"Trust in the Lord, and do good; so shalt thou dwell in the land and verily thou shalt be fed. Delight thyself also in the Lord: and he shall give thee the desires of thine heart. Commit thy way unto the Lord; trust also in him; and he shall bring it to pass." (Psalm 37:3-5 KJV)

BODY

"Therefore, I urge you, brothers and sisters, in view of God's mercy, to offer your bodies as a living sacrifice, holy and pleasing to God—this is your true and proper worship." (Romans 12:1 NIV)

"Sexual sins and neglecting the law of purity in the body of Christ is an element that can bring weakness, sickness, and even premature death in the church. It's a forgotten aspect of not discerning the Lord's body, like when one participates in the Holy Communion unworthily. (1Cor. 11:29-31 NIV)

The previous statements sound primitive in today's contemporary church. There is a lack of ministry from pastors (as a whole) in the area of sexual sins.

In the days of old it was common for correction to be made by using scripture and by the manifestation of the gifts of the Holy Spirit. It was understood that only deep repentance and cleansing through the precious blood of Jesus could sexual sins be pardoned." (Charismanews. com The Flaming Herald by Bert Farias / Why Sexual Sin is Weakening the Body of Christ)

"In the books of the Mosaic Law we find references to sexual immorality and nakedness.

The first recorded human curse was over nakedness (Gen.9:20-23 KJV).

Almost two chapters in the Old Testament has reference to a code of ethics on nakedness and sexual immorality (Lev.18 and 20 KJV).

When Moses came down from the mountain from receiving the commandment from the Lord, the people were worshiping a golden calf, "unrestrained" (New King James version). The (King James) version says: they were "naked," and the (Living Bible) says, "committing adultery." (Ex. 32:25 KJV). And all this happened shortly after a move of God.

A key to overcoming sexual sin is to meditate on God's Word concerning them. It nurtures the fear of the Lord in you. In (Gal. 5:19-21 KJV) sexual sin is listed first in the works of the flesh. The first four sexual sins in the King James version are: Adultery, fornication, uncleanness, lasciviousness; The first sexual sins in the Amplified version are: sexual immorality, impurity, sensuality (total irresponsibility, lack of self-control). Sexual sin is listed not only here, but also in several other scriptural references in the New testament.

Sexual Sin Reference Scriptures:

- (Romans 1:24; 6:19) – Uncleanness is singled out.
- (1 Cor.6:9-11) – Sexual sins listed first.
- (Galatians 5: 19-21) – Sexual sins listed first.
- (Ephesians 4:19) – Lewdness and uncleanness singled out.
- (Ephesians 5:3) – Fornication and uncleanness singled out.
- (Colossians 3:5) – Fornication and uncleanness listed first.
- (1Thessalonians 4:3) – Sexual immorality singled out in our walk of sanctification.
- (1 Peter 4:3) – Lewdness listed first from our past life."

(www.charismanews.com >The Flaming Herald By Bert Farias / 4 Sexual Sins Every Christian Should Avoid)

This is serious business; the devil is not your friend and your flesh is an enemy to God. If you are having a problem in this area of your life, get Some Help!

Need Help? Talk to your pastor, or a faith-based counselor. Go online and type in free help for Sexual Addition. The internet offers several faith-based listings for you to consider.

The Holy Bible says: "It is actually reported that there is sexual immorality among you, and of a kind that even pagans do not tolerate: A man is sleeping with his father's wife." (1 Corinthians 5:1 NIV) "Do you not know that your bodies are members of Christ himself? Shall I then take the members of Christ and unite them with a prostitute? Never! Do you not know that he who unites himself with a prostitute is one with her in body? For it is said, "The two will become one flesh." But whoever is united with the Lord is one with him in spirit. Flee from sexual immorality. All other sins a person commits are outside the body, but whoever sins sexually, sins against their own body. Do you not know that your bodies are temples of the Holy Spirit, who is in you, whom you have received from God? You are not your own; you were bought at a price. Therefore honor God with your bodies." (1 Corinthians 6:15-20 NIV)

Sex outside of marriage dishonors God

"Now, about sex and marriage: Drink only the water that comes from your own well, and don't let your water flow out into the streets. Keep it for yourself, and don't share it with strangers. Be happy with your own wife. Enjoy the woman you married while you were young. She is like a beautiful deer, a lovely fawn. Let her love satisfy you completely. Stay drunk on her love, and don't go stumbling into the arms another woman." (Proverbs 5:15-20 ERV)

Our world is too consumed with sex. Television promotes all kinds of sexual immorality. Even the commercials are promoting sensuality.

Women are being degraded in selling under garments, and people have become so desensitized to the degradation that it is readily accepted.

Even chewing gum may show someone putting a stick of gum in their mouth just before a kiss, giving the impression that the gum is going to make the kiss so much better. And of course, everyone wants a kiss to be sweet and lasting, so buy this brand of gum. Lingerie companies have young beautiful women, modeling matching bra and panties, knowing that men are creatures of sight. They may envision their wife or girlfriend in that set of underwear and make the purchase. Young single women with enticing motives select provocative lingerie to display in front of their boyfriends. Is the main focus to promote sex?

My Family and I went to a beach in Sandestin, while living in Florida. One of my sons who was about three years old at the time, saw a young lady in a bikini bathing suit. He wanted me to see this young lady because he said she was in her underwear. He didn't realize that the young lady was wearing a swimsuit. In his mind they looked like underwear. In actuality it took about the same amount of material to make that bikini as it would a brassiere and a pair of panties.

Where is our shame? The more nakedness we can uncover the sexier we feel.

A close relationship, wisdom, and a surrendered body to the Lord, can and will be a help against the temptation to sin sexually. That is not to say that the urge will not exist, but it is to say, that God will give you power to resist. And if one can furnish the faith and ask him, the Lord can even take the desire away. My husband went overseas for twelve months and the Lord kept us. He was in Korea, where many of the women are beautiful and enticing. They target military men, and many fall under their spell. Families are broken up, emotions are crushed, and fathers are divorced from their families. In the country of Korea the Mamasan will come up to the military men and invite them to come and get a pretty girl. My husband was approached, and he showed mamasan his wedding ring and announced, "I have a pretty girl." The temptation can be great when you are away from your family, lonely and enticed by a beautiful women. But thank God, "He is able to keep you from stumbling or falling into sin!" (Jude 1:24(a) AMP) The enemy is trying to destroy families through a spirit of sexual immorality. Instead of unity, we see a spirit of division in the family. This is not God's plan for humanity. God made male and female to be fruitful and replenish the earth, giving them joy in the process. A reproduction which was not just natural but also one of the spirit. Believers are to be a light in this world's darkness, and instruments of light reproduction. We must live in a way that people will see God at work and give Him praise. Hopefully wanting to emulate what they see.

Health and Healing – Dr. Walt Larimore

Doctor Larimore states: "God is concerned about our health." Many nonphysical factors play an important role in the development of certain illnesses."

Paul prayed that the believers "whole self – spirit, soul, and body – will be kept safe and be blameless when our Lord Jesus Christ comes." (1Thessalonians 5:23 ERV) Health for the whole man is known as Holistic health. It is the care for one's physical, mental, spiritual, and social needs. Each facet affects overall health, and ailing in one part affects others. (https://dignityhealth.org.articles What is Holistic Health Care Anyway)

"The following passages show some of the ways in which holistic health is taught throughout the Bible:

- Emotions are linked to health, as in (Proverbs 17:22 NIV) "A cheerful heart is good medicine, but a crushed spirit dries up the bones."
- Health is influenced by the morality of our actions: "For those who eat and drink without discerning the body of the Christ

eat and drink judgement on themselves. That is why many among you are weak and sick, and a number of you have fallen asleep." (1 Corinthians 11:29-30 NIV)

• Our spiritual vitality is linked to our health: "Dear friend, I pray that you may enjoy good health and that all may go well with you, even as your soul is getting along well. (3 John 2 NIV)

Do not be wise in your own eyes; fear the Lord and shun evil. This will bring health to your body and nourishment to your bones." (Proverb 3:7-8 NIV; Deuteronomy 30:15-16 NIV)

(www.drwalt.com Faith-Based Health and Healing – Part 1 – What Does the Bible Say About Health? Dr. Walt Larimore To a Healthier You)

Healthy Eating Scriptures (all in English Standard Version)

1. (1 Corinthians 10:31) "So, Whether you eat or drink, or whatever you do, do all to the glory of God."
2. (Genesis 1:29) And God said, "Behold, I have given you every plant yielding seed that is on the face of all the earth, and every tree with seed in its fruit. You shall have them for food."
3. (1 Corinthians 9:27) "But I discipline my body and keep it under control, lest after preaching to other I myself should be disqualified."
4. (3 John 1:2) "Beloved, I pray that all may go well with you and that you may be in good health, as it goes well with your soul. (www.openbible.info>topics> healthy eating)

PARENTS

Children obey your parents in the Lord, for this is right. Honor your father and mother"—which is the first commandment with a promise—so that it may go well with you and that you may enjoy long life on the earth." (Ephesians 6:1-3 NIV)

God has given parents authority to govern and shape the lives of their children. They are due respect because of the level of responsibility they carry. The understanding parents acquire, comes through experience. Our offspring have not developed to that degree of maturity. Many difficulties in life they would not have to encounter, if they would listen, and apply the sound judgement of their parents.

Thank God for godly examples of parents in the Word of God. The Bible tells us to treat the elder men as fathers and the elder women as mothers. (1Tim. 5:1-2 KJV)

The book of Titus lets us know that the aged men and women have a responsibility to be an example of holiness; that they may teach the younger Christians, how to live a life pleasing unto the Lord. (Titus 2:1-8 KJV)

Showing respect to others honors God

As Micah looked at his society it grieved him. He didn't see many godly people: he saw corruption, people killing each other, officials taking bribes, judges taking money, violence and immorality. We see in the verses below; family love was almost nonexistent. How do we see our world today? Who is honoring God?

"For a son dishonors his father, a daughter rises up against her mother, a daughter-in-law against her mother-in-law. A man's enemies are the men (members) of his own household. But as for me, I watch in hope for the Lord, I wait for God my Savior; my God will hear me." (Micah 7:6-7 NIV)

"Children, obey your parents [as God's representatives] in all things, for this [attitude of respect and obedience] is well-pleasing to the Lord [and will bring you God's promised blessings]." (Colossians 3:20 AMP)

Consequences of dishonoring parents

"Honor (respect, obey, care for) your father and your mother, so that your days may be prolonged in the land the Lord your God gives you." (Exodus 20:12 AMP)

Years ago, in my early twenties (I didn't know the Lord at that time) I took a trip to Ohio with a young man who I called my boyfriend. My mother begged me not to go but I went anyway. I was in a car accident with this young man and incurred injuries while my boyfriend did not get hurt at all. God sometimes give parents intuition concerning their children. And it would be wise to listen and obey. Strive to please God: Goodness and Mercy will follow!

Instructions to the heads of the family

We honor God by treating our children right.

"Father's do not provoke your children to anger [do not exasperate them to the point of resentment with demands that are trivial of unreasonable or humiliating or abusive; nor by showing favoritism or indifference to any of them], but bring them up [tenderly, with lovingkindness] in the discipline and instruction of the Lord." (Ephesians 6:4 AMP)

Children look to parents for examples of behavior. We are the first examples they see. So it behooves us to be a great example. Often, we want children to do what we say and not what we do. But the reality is they will do what they see you do. I saw a movie entitled "42", The Jackie Robinson Story.

"In 1947, Jackie Robinson becomes the first African-American to play in Major League Baseball in the modern era when he was signed by the Brooklyn Dodgers and faces considerable racism in the process." (https://www.imdb.com.title 42 – 2013)

In that movie a young Caucasian boy went to a baseball game where Jackie Robinson was playing, he was so excited, he began to cheer until he looked at his father. His father along with others started booing and shouting out racial slurs. And that young boy who was once cheering began to boo and shout ugly names as well.

How wonderful the world would be if our actions were out of love and not hate, out of kindness and not bitterness with a mutual respect for all humanity.

UNITY

Apostle Paul pleaded with the church at Corinth.

"I appeal to you, brothers and sisters, in the name our Lord Jesus Christ, that all of you agree with one another in what you say and that there be no divisions among you, but that you be perfectly united in mind and thought."(1Corinthians 1:10 NIV)

Fighting and quarreling among believers does not honor God.

"Two people are better than one. When two people work together, they get more work done. If one person falls, the other person can reach out to help. But those who are alone when they fall have no one to help them. If two people sleep together, they will be warm. But a person sleeping alone will not be warm. An enemy might be able to defeat one person, but two people can stand back-to-back to defend each other. And three people are even stronger. They are like a rope that has three parts wrapped together - it is very hard to break." (Ecclesiastes 4:9-12 ERV)

"Submit Yourselves to God"

"What causes fights and quarrels among you? Don't they come from your desires that battle within you? You desire but do not have, so you kill. You covet but you cannot get what you want, so you quarrel and fight. You do not have because you do not ask God. When you ask, you do not receive, because you ask with wrong motives, that you may spend what you get on your pleasures. You adulterous people, don't you know that friendship with world means enmity against God? Therefore anyone who chooses to be a friend of the world becomes an enemy of God." (James 4:1-4 NIV)

Come on, examine your actions, agree with God's word, and repent. Allow change to take place in your life and be an example for others to follow.

"Put to death, therefore whatever belongs to your earthly nature: sexual immorality, impurity, lust, evil desires and greed, which is idolatry. Because of these, the wrath of God is coming. Therefore, as God's chosen people, holy and dearly loved, clothe yourselves with compassion, kindness, humility, gentleness and patience. Bear with each other and forgive one another if any of you has a grievance against someone. Forgive as the Lord forgave you. And over all these virtues put on love, which binds them all together in perfect unity. Let the peace of Christ rule in your hearts, since as members of one body you were called to peace. And be thankful." (Colossians 3:5-6, 12-15 NIV)

These scriptures are a full course meal for the soul. Digesting the meat of this word and letting its nutrients empower your being, produces unity with God and each other.

PART FOUR

What's That Smell?

**OF THE FIVE SENSES,
SMELL IS THE ONE WITH
THE BEST MEMORY**
Rebecca McClanahan

AROMA

"I identified myself completely with Him. Indeed, I have been crucified with Christ. My ego is no longer central. It is no longer important that I appear righteous before you or have your good opinion, and I am no longer driven to impress God. Christ lives in me. The life you see me living is not "mine," but it is lived by faith in the Son of God, who loved me and gave himself for me. I am not going to go back on that." (Galatians 2:20 MSG)

The Shape of Maturity

When children start developing physically you see the signs. Girls and boys grow pubic hairs, bodies start changing and attitudes change. A façade of adulthood seems to cloud their thinking. Their actions suggest, they think they have a right to talk to adults on the same level. Many times they speak in a disrespectful tone, manifesting a need for correction. All adults, especially parents should know, it takes more than physical growth to be mature. Mark Merrill featured Dr. Tim Elmore on his blog entitled: "Helping Families Love Well." Dr. Elmore shared seven marks of maturity in the book "Generation iY: Our Last Chance to Save Their Future." This article gives us a glimpse into the character of a mature person.

Seven Marks of Maturity by Dr. Tim Elmore

1. **"A mature person is able to keep long-term commitments.**
   a. The ability to delay gratification.
   b. Able to keep commitments even when they don't feel like it.
2. **A mature person is unshaken by flattery or criticism.**
   a. Understanding that nothing is as good or bad as it seems.
   b. Can receive compliments or criticism without letting it ruin them.
3. **A mature person possesses a spirit of humility.**
   a. Doesn't think less of themselves, but think about themselves less.
   b. Honors the Creator who gave them their talent and potential.
4. **A mature person's decisions are based on character, not feelings.**
   a. Have principles that guide their decision.
   b. Their character is master over their emotions.
5. **A mature person expresses gratitude consistently.**
   a. Grateful for big and little things in life
   b. Mature sees the big picture and realize they have it good compared to most of the world's population.
6. **A mature person knows how to prioritize others before themselves.**
   a. Ability to get past one's own desires.
   b. Considers the needs of others.
7. **A mature person seeks wisdom before acting.**
   a. Mature people are teachable.
   b. Seeks counsel from the more experienced, dependable friends, or from God in prayer."

Self-Examination!

The truth of the matter is there is always room for growth.

In life one may find themselves challenged emotionally. Your name may be spoken negatively on the lips of others. Rejection and alienation may cause you to think that you are unloved and alone. Feelings of detachment may flood your soul, and the battle of isolation begins. Thoughts may race through your mind like: I don't need this; I'll be just fine by myself. But the reality is: we are the body of Christ, and every part is necessary. Overcoming challenges is a testimony to our connection and maturity in the risen Savior. Security in Christ must be one's stability when challenges come. The question is: will I be strong or cower under pressure? What do you do when your emotions want to go opposite of God's way? You follow God! Sometimes that means relying on the strength and prayers of others.

What about that Noah?

Noah sacrificed only clean animals on the altar. This was an act of humility, faith and devotion. Regardless of his feelings, he chose to follow God's instructions. He believed the almighty had spoken, and acted upon His word. Noah was devoted to obeying the Father. God smelled the smoke from the sacrifice, as an aroma of Noah's character. His respect and love for the Creator was a sweet fragrance to Him.

The Fire

Where there is smoke there is fire! "Fire represents many things to many people and cultures. It's recognized as a purifier, a destroyer and as the generative power of life, energy and change. It represents illumination and enlightenment, destruction and renewal, spirituality and damnation." (https://ww.ukessays.com)

In ancient Israel, fire is taken literally in several hundred references. The proof of the figurative manifestation of God's being or actions is also a large number. (Fire Definition biblestudytools.com)

"The laws in the book of Leviticus form part of a historical narrative. Showing how Israel became a nation, and what was involved in being called God's people. God's covenant purpose, to make them "a kingdom of priests, and a holy nation" (Exodus 19:6 KJV) was worked out in an all-embracing system of religious services, and social laws." (Introduction to Leviticus – King James Study Bible pg.169)

The first chapter talks about the Law of the Burnt Offering which was a sacrifice for sin. "The worshiper would bring an animal to the priest. It would be completely burned, and none eaten. It was totally given to the Lord. It was very costly, because meat was a rare luxury in that time. The worshiper put his hands on the head of the animal which was a declaration that the animal was carrying his sins and was dying in his stead. The burnt sacrifice was offered to satisfy God's wrath (against sin) under the old covenant." (2 Chronicles 29:7-8 The Burnt Offering | Reformed Bible Studies & Devotion liqonier.org)

"He shall lay his hand on the head of the burnt offering [transferring symbolically his guilt to the sacrifice], that it may be accepted for him to make atonement on his behalf." (Leviticus 1:5 AMP) In the thirteenth verse: "The priest shall offer all of it, and offer it up in smoke on the altar. It is a burnt offering, an offering by fire, a sweet and soothing aroma to the Lord." (Leviticus 1:13 AMP)

The New Testament speaks to the Christian to make oneself a present to God in holiness.

"I beseech you therefore brethren by the mercies of God that you present your body a living sacrifice holy acceptable unto God which is your reasonable service. And be not conformed to this world but be ye transformed by the renewing of your mind, that ye may prove what is that good, and acceptable, and perfect, will of God." (Roman 12:1-2 KJV)

Your body must be put on the altar of sacrifice to be purified. There must be a destroying of the outer man (flesh). How does God do this? Fiery trials! Peter said: "Friends when life gets really difficult, don't jump to the conclusion that God isn't on the job. Instead, be glad that you are in the thick of what Christ experienced. This is a spiritual refining process, with glory just around the corner." (1Peter 4:12-13 MSG)

In (Isaiah 53:10 AMP) The prophet speaks of Christ: "Yet the Lord was willing to crush Him, causing Him to suffer; If He would give Himself as a guilt offering [an atonement for sin], He shall see His [spiritual] offspring, He shall prolong His days, and the will (good pleasure) of the Lord shall succeed and prosper in His hand."

"He made Christ who knew no sin to [judicially] be sin on our behalf, so that in Him we would become the righteousness of God [that is, we would be made acceptable to Him and placed in a right relationship with Him by His gracious lovingkindness]."(2Cor. 5:21AMP) Thank God for Jesus!

The Work

First Corinthians the third chapter talks about building the foundation of Christ.

"But if anyone builds on the foundation with gold, silver, precious stones, wood, hay, straw, each one's work will be clearly shown [for what it is]; for the day [of judgment] will disclose it, because it is to be revealed with fire, and the fire will test the quality and character and worth of each person's work. If any person's work which he has built [on this foundation, that is any outcome of his effort] remains [and survives this test], he will receive a reward." (1 Corinthians 3:12-14 AMP)

Let us not offer to God strange fire. Nadab and Abihu, Aaron's sons offered strange fire (unauthorized fire, contrary to His command) unto God to their destruction. (Leviticus 10:1-2 ERV) "Then Aaron's sons Nadab and Abihu made a mistake. They took their incense dishes and put some fire and incense in them. But they did not use the fire on the altar- they took fire from some other place and brought it to the Lord." "It was a sign of their disregard for the utter holiness of God and the need to honor and obey Him in solemn and holy fear. Their carelessness and irreverence were their downfall." (Leviticus, New International Commentary on the Old Testament by Gordon Wenham Got Questions) When the Ministers of church sin and dishonor God, it hurts their witness, and causes people to distrust the reality of Christ.

I was blessed to be in a church service where Mother Annie M. Cooper, (the former Texas Southwest supervisor of Women), was the guest speaker.

I came alone that night, which I very seldom do. What I did not know, and now am assured of is, the Lord wanted to speak to me concerning Aroma. During the drive home the Holy Spirit began to teach me that congregations have (a spiritual redolence), a strong smell or fragrance. It's a distinctive quality that's picked up in one's spirit. Have you ever arrived at a church and before you could get in the building good, you felt an exhilaration? The kind of excitement that ushered you inside and catches you up in worship. That atmosphere usually comes from a praying leader, who teaches those under his/her leadership the importance and power of prayer. Because it is not only taught but acted upon, there is a consistent aromatic experience when one comes into its presence.

To give some clarity to what I'm talking about, let's look briefly at what Aromatherapy is all about. "It is a practice of using natural oils from bark, stems, leaves, and roots to enhance psychological and physical well-being. When one inhales the aroma it's believed that it stimulates brain function. These oils can also be absorbed through the skin, travel through the bloodstream and promote whole-body healing." (http://www.aromatherapy.com) So when one learns these holistic methods and shares it with others, they can receive the same benefits.

It reminds me of (Psalm 133:1-3 AMP) "How good and how pleasant for brothers to dwell together in unity! It is like the precious oil [of consecration] poured upon the head, coming down on the beard, even the beard on Aaron, coming down upon the edge of his [priestly] robes [consecrating the whole body]. It is like the dew of [Mount] Hermon coming down on the hills of Zion; for there the Lord has commanded the blessing: life forevermore." God's holy oil consecrated the whole body. In the same way the anointing that is on the leader, flows to the congregation. If one is observant, it can be recognized. Because we are God's children there is a certain aura that we carry.

That aroma is a fragrant life. A life connected to Him in obedience. A fragrance that is only obtained through a surrendered life. A life lived through God's Holy Spirit and worked out by faith. It's a relationship of trust. The believer's trust in God is demonstrated by his or her compliance to His will. Our heavenly Father knows His children, entrust us with responsibilities and blessings according to what we can handle. His primary goal is to cause one to mature and take on the image of Christ, enabling one to draw others into the kingdom. Lost souls will receive life and our enemy the devil will be defeated.

This kind of life solidifies a love relationship with the Father. God shows His love for us by drawing us to Himself. We show our love to Him by coming to Him in obedient surrender. "No one can come to Me unless the Father who sent Me draws him [giving him the desire to come to Me]; and I will raise him up [from the dead] on the last day." (John 6:44 AMP) God opened a way for us to have a personal relationship with Him through the death of His son Jesus Christ. "For God so [greatly] loved and dearly prized the world, that He [even] gave His [One and] only begotten Son, so that whoever believes and trusts in Him [as Savior] shall not perish, but have eternal life." (John 3:16 AMP) We love The Lord because He first loved us. What an awesome privilege to love and be loved by the Creator, and to know that the Almighty God is ever present, suppling our needs and giving us peace.

The believer who trusts Jesus as Savior is a light to humanity that sits in darkness. He/she is a remedy for a sin sick world, who would otherwise be eternally separated from the Father. One who sees the light in a believer and buys into it can have the same illumination. To buy into the light is to desire it, to invest in it, and to receive the light of Jesus into ones heart. One of our Bible study lessons stated: "That in the name of Jesus, we have the power to bind up the brokenness in people, and release healing power into the heart and mind of the deeply depressed." People are going to doctors, hospitals, clinics, and psychiatrist receiving therapy to get help for their condition, believing that's their only hope. But the born-again believer offers hope. We have therapeutic benefits that promote well-being. It's the power in the blood of Jesus Christ, the healing truth of God's Word and the results of working that Word in our lives by faith. The prophet Isaiah said: "He will guard him and keep him in perfect and constant peace whose mind [both its inclination and its character] is stayed on Him and hope confidently in Him." (Isaiah 26:3 AMP)

THE FRAGRANT ENVIRONMENT

"But thanks be to God, who always leads us in triumph in Christ, and through us spreads and makes evident everywhere the sweet fragrance of the knowledge of Him. For we are the sweet fragrance of Christ [which ascends] to God, [discernible both] among those who are being saved and among those who are perishing; to the latter one an aroma from death to death [a fatal, offensive odor], but to the other an aroma from life to life [a vital fragrance, living and fresh]. And who is adequate and sufficiently qualified for these things? For we are not like many, [acting like merchant] peddling God's word [shortchanging and adulterating God's message]; but from pure [uncompromised] motives, as [commissioned and sent] from God, we speak [His message in Christ in the sight of God." (2 Cor. 2:14-17 AMP)

As believers we were born to be a life-giving fragrance. The ones who reject God may see Christians as a deadly fragrance. Simply because they refuse to give up their sinful ways. Many are hearers of God's Word but refused to receive its message.

They bring upon themselves the penalty of their sins which is death (eternal separation from God).

Mike Murdock said in his book "Seeds of Wisdom on the Word of God,"

"The very presence of a Bible often produces as aura and change in the atmosphere." As I pondered this in my mind; I concluded that if the physical appearance of the Bible changes the atmosphere; then certainly there will be an atmospheric change by the spoken Word of God. It will affect all that believe and receive the word. Mr. Murdock also gave eleven reasons why the Bible is the most important book on earth:

1. It is the Wisdom of God
2. It is the Love Book of the Universe
3. It is a Book on Order
4. It Reveals the Laws of the Universe
5. It is a Relationship Handbook
6. It is a Worship Encyclopedia
7. It Teaches Spiritual Protocol
8. It is a Problem-Solving Handbook
9. It is a Deliverance Handbook for the Captives
10. It Creates Conviction that Causes Change.
11. It is the Book of Divine Secrets.

This world is in a state of chaos due to humanities irreverence of God's book of order. Society needs order if we are going to survive. God's order brings peace to individuals as well as nations if followed. When one goes about on his or her own feelings; complete disorder and confusion is manifested. 'Every way of a man is right in his own eyes: but the Lord pondereth the hearts." (Proverb 21:2 KJV) God's wisdom book will help us in our everyday decision making. Solomon the wisest man who ever lived writes in the second chapter of Proverbs.

"Listen to wisdom, and do your best to understand. Ask for good judgment. Cry out for understanding. Look for wisdom like silver. Search for it like hidden treasure. If you do this, you will understand what it means to respect the Lord, and you will come to know God. Planning ahead will protect you, and understanding will guard you. These will keep you from following the wrong path and will protect you from those who have evil plans." (Proverbs 2:2-5, 11-12 ERV)

THE ATTITUDE OF THE HEART

Walk into a room where there have been sharp words, and individuals are angry. with each other; you can feel the tension in the atmosphere. The attitude of one's heart produces a fragrance before God and a life changing effect on those in its environment. Bad attitudes will have a negative effect on others. Individuals as well as associates will benefit from the heart of one with faith, love and obedience towards God. When one desires to walk close to God it will be manifested in personal prayer time. Because of that relationship he/she will gladly give to others.

In (Phil.4:17-19 AMP) Paul was thanking the Philippians for their sacrificial giving. He said: "Not that I seek the gift itself, but I do seek the profit which increases to your [heavenly] account [the blessing which is accumulation for you]. But I have received everything in full and more; I am amply supplied, having received from Epaphroditus the gifts you sent me. They are the fragrant aroma of an offering, an acceptable sacrifice which God welcomes and in which He delights. And my God will liberally supply (fill until full) your every need according to His riches in glory in Christ Jesus."

When one gives to support God's messengers, it is like giving directly to God. Our gifts are a fragrant offering, pleasing to God. He touches the hearts of men and causes them to give to you. Our needs will be met as we remain faithful to Him and give to others. The Philippians faithfulness to help others brought God's blessings into their lives. (Philippians 4:16, 19 Fire Bible notes pg. 2284)

"Then Mary took about a pint of pure nard, an expensive perfume; she poured it on Jesus' feet and wiped his feet with her hair. And the house was filled with the fragrance of the perfume." (John 12:3 NIV)

Can you see the heart of Mary! She takes this expensive perfume and pours it on Jesus's feet and wipes His feet with her hair. Her actions revealed sacrifice, an expression of reverence and adoration for the Lord.

When one's life is perfumed with love, people in the mist will reap the benefits.

I have seen people blessed by a fragrant life. People have been saved, healed, and delivered due to the life of a believer who was devoted to God. I came to know the Lord because of the life of my mother-in-love, Willie Mae Johnson.

People of God, it is no time to take down. Stand up and be the people, God is calling for in these last days.

The Now Generation and those to follow need to see the light of God's love shining through the church. How will they know what it looks like, and be drawn to it, unless they see it in the believer? Shine people of God Shine!

"Let your light so shine before men, that they may see your good works, and glorify your Father which is in heaven." (Matthew 5:16 KJV)

Asaph in Psalm 78 reflects on Israel's history, and expresses the main point of the Psalm. Which is to know God, put hope in Him, forget not His deeds and obey His commandments.

"He decreed statutes for Jacob and established the law in Israel, which he commanded our ancestors to teach their children, so the next generation would know them, even the children yet to be born, and they in turn would tell their children. Then they would put their trust in God and would not forget his deeds but would keep his commands." (Psalm 78:5-7 NIV)

When devoted believers pray, that aroma is like fragrant spices to the Lord.

"And when he had taken the scroll, the four living creatures and the twenty-four elders (of the heavenly Sanhedrin) prostrated themselves before the Lamb. Each was holding a harp (lute or guitar), and they both had golden bowls full of incense (fragrant spices and gums for burning), which are the prayers of God's people (the saints)." (Revelation 5:8 AMP)

The Lord put this declaration in my spirit several years ago. It has been there every sense:

"We are not praying in vain, but we are praying with purpose, with results.

If we ask it shall be given, if we seek, we shall find, if we knock the door shall, be open unto us. (Matthew 7:7 KJV)

And we have this confidence in Him. That if we ask anything according to His will, He hears us, and we know that if He hear us, we have the request that we desire of Him. And we receive of Him because we keep His commandments and do those things that are pleasing in His sight." (1John 5:14-15; 3:22 KJV)

May we have a heart to obey God's Command and do what pleases Him.

DEVELOPING GODLY CHARACTER

"Good character is more to be praised than outstanding talent. Most talents are, to some extent, a gift. Good character, by contrast, is not given to us. We have to build it piece by piece, by thought, choice, courage and determination." Quote Tab >quotes by-John Luther

To produce a fragrant environment one must build and exemplify Godly character.

Joyce Meyer said: "We develop Godly Character when we treat people the way we want to be treated, not the way they may treat us." (Pinterest 300 Joyce Meyer-Inspirations)

"We have to watch our thoughts because they become words. Watch our words because they become actions. Watch our actions because they become habits. Watch our habits because they become character. Watch your character because it will become your destiny." (quote by Lao Tzu https://www.goodreads.com/quotes/8203490-watch-your-thoughts-they become-your-words-watch-your-words)

"One will only begin to develop godly character when we're in Christ, and we place faith in Him to bring us victoriously through the trails of life."

(ourdailyjourney.beta.ourdailybread.org / Developing Godly Character submitted by Pastor Asa Dockery)

"Therefore, since we have been justified [that is, acquitted of sin, declared blameless before God] by faith, [let us grasp the fact that] we have peace with God [and the joy of reconciliation with Him] through our Lord Jesus Christ (the Messiah, the Anointed). ³ And not only *this*, but [with joy] let us exult in our sufferings *and* rejoice in our hardships, knowing that hardship (distress, pressure, trouble) produces patient endurance; ⁴ and endurance, proven character (spiritual maturity); and proven character, hope *and* confident assurance [of eternal salvation]." (Romans 5:1, 3-4 AMP)

A STENCH IN GOD'S NOSTRILS

Odors which are strong and very unpleasant (stenches) often time affect our surroundings. "Unpleasant odors can be a warning sign of potential risk to human health. Odors from environmental sources might also cause health symptoms, depending on the physical state of individuals and environmental factors."

(www.atsdr.cdc.gov>air_pollution_odor_diaries)

Spiritual lessons can be learned from observing natural phenomenon.

Sin is an unpleasant odor to God. It can present itself in various ways; like hatred, envy, strife, bitterness and unforgiveness towards one another. These displays of emotion smell bad to God and produces a negative affect in the lives of others.

In the third chapter of Isaiah, the prophet tells of future desolations that will come upon Judah and Jerusalem for their sins. God threatens, to deprive them of all supports both of life and government. To leave them to fall into confusion and disorder. To deny them the blessing of judicial officers. To strip the daughters of Zion of their ornaments. To lay all waste by the sword of war. The sins that provoked God was, their bold disobedience, their disregard for others, the abuse of power to oppression and cruel government rule. And the pride of the daughters of Zion. In spite of general calamities, God assured good people that it should be well with them. And wicked people that, it will go ill with them. If only nations of the earth, would hearken to the rebukes and warnings of this chapter. (Isaiah 3: 1-26 KJV Matthew Henry Bible Commentary (complete) www.christianity.com)

"As a result of the people's rebellion and rejection of God, his judgement would touch every part of society; and all classes of people would suffer." (Isa. 3 vv.2-3 NIV Fire Bible Notes Global Addition)

God, who is the giver, said I am taking from you. At that particular time in history they were a divided kingdom. Israel had already been conquered and destroyed by Assyria. And God was warning Judah that the same thing was going to happen to them.

"The Lord God All-Powerful will take away everything Judah and Jerusalem depend on. He will take away all the food and water. He will take away all the heroes and soldiers. He will take away all the judges, the prophets, the fortunetellers, and the elders. He will take away the army officers and important officials. He will take away the skilled counselors, the magicians, and those who try to tell the future." (Isaiah 3:1-3 ERV)

"When a society rejects God's ways, it opens the way for injustice, cruelty and violence. In this type of social environment, rebellion against parents and other authorities is common among youth. People slowly lose moral restraint. People refuse to control their behavior or take responsibility for their actions. Because of the rebellious attitude and actions, the society falls apart. (Isa.vv.5)

God told Isaiah to encourage those who remained faithful even when others continued to defy God and behave wickedly. In such a spiritually hostile environment, people will often suffer for doing what is right; but God promised to take care of his people." (Isaiah 3:1-10 NIV Fire Bible Notes Global Addition pg. 1155)

In (Isaiah 3:16-26 NIV) the behavior of the daughters of Zion were a stench in God's nostrils.

"The Lord says, "The daughters of Zion are haughty, walking along with outstretched necks, flirting with eyes, strutting along with swaying hips, with ornaments jingling on their ankles. Therefore the Lord will bring sores on the heads of the women of Zion; the Lord will make their scalps bald."

"Instead of fragrance there will be a stench; instead of a sash, a rope; instead of well-dressed hair, baldness; instead of fine clothing, sackcloth; instead of beauty, branding." (Isaiah 3:16-17; 24 NIV)

These Old Testament woman paid more attention to their outer appearance than to inner beauty. They were not interested in reflecting the Father's love through godly character. But were self-centered and obsessed with beauty and being sexually attractive. There was no concern for the poor, oppressed or the spiritually impoverished condition of their families. And because of this, God said He was going to allow them to experience shame and disgrace. When their enemies conquered them, they would become slaves. (Isaiah 3 16-26 NIV Fire Bible notes – Global Study Addition)

God demands humility, modesty and holiness.

Questions arose in my mind, why would God pick on women? What kind of responsibility have been given us? Are we now or have been careless with that entrustment? "Women were created to be a loving companion and helper for man. Sharing in responsibility and cooperating with each other to fulfill God's purpose." (Fire Bible Global Study Edition notes Gen 2:18 pg.36)

As I pondered on the scripture in Isaiah and other women in the Bible it was apparent to me, some have misappropriated the use of trust. God has given women the power of influence. And men have fallen under the power of devious women throughout history. Like Eve with Adam, multiple wives with Solomon, Jezebel with Ahab, and Delilah with Samson. A more productive use of influence would be to think less of oneself and more of the assignment to help.

The New Testament warns against the same kind of attitude in women.

"Your adornment must not be merely external – with interweaving and elaborate knotting of the hair, and wearing gold jewelry, or [being superficially preoccupied with] dressing in expensive clothes; but let it be [the inner beauty of] the hidden person of the heart, with the imperishable quality and unfading charm of a gentle and peaceful spirit, [one that is calm and self-controlled, not overanxious, but serene and spiritually mature] which is very precious in the sight of God." (1 Peter 3:3-4 AMP)

Women usually like to look good and smell good, and that's ok. What God is interested in, is the condition of one's heart. Let us not look like millionaires on the outside and paupers on the inside. Godly women you are so beautiful, needed and important to the Body of Christ and humanity. Invest the time to keep that inner self immaculate. When The Father inhales the fragrance of your heart it will be such a sweet aroma that it will make Him smile. *Come on, let us make God smile!*

THE SPIRIT OF THIS AGE

"The characteristics of an era which dominate the thinking of the massed" Harold Vaughn.

Paul said in (Romans 12:2 ERV): "Don't change yourself to be like the people of this world, but be what God wants for you. You will be able to know what is good and pleasing to him and what is perfect."

The world and its system of thinking is not in accordance with God's Word. The world is not subject to the will of God nor can it be. If a believer says he/she loves God and follows after the dictate of the world; they are not telling the truth. "Love not the world neither the things that are in the world. If any man love the world, the love of the Father is not in him. For all that is in the world, the lust of the flesh, and the lust of the eyes, and the pride of life, is not of the Father, but is of the world. And the world passeth away, and the lust thereof: but he that doeth the will of God abideth forever." (1 John 2:15-17 KJV)

Apostle Paul reminds believers of worldly influence that affected their decisions before excepting Christ. That same spirit of the world is at work today.

"And you [He made alive when you] were [spiritually] dead and separated from Him because of your transgressions and sins, in which you once walked.

You were following the ways of this world [influenced by this present age], in accordance with the prince of the power of the air (Satan), the spirit who is now at work in the disobedient [the unbelieving, who fight against the purpose of God].

Among these [unbelievers] we all once lived in the passions of our flesh [our behavior governed by the sinful self], indulging the desires of human nature [without the Holy Spirit] and [the impulses] of the [sinful] mind. We were, by nature, children [under the sentence] of God's wrath, just like the rest [of mankind]. (Ephesians 2:1-3 AMP)

"So be alert [give strict attention, be cautious and active in faith], for you do not know in what kind of a day [whether near or far] your Lord is coming." (Matt. 24:42 AMP) Beginning with Matthew the twenty forth chapter and the thirty-seventh verse it states: "that when the son of man comes, it will be like the days of Noah. Men and women will be eating and drinking marrying and giving their children to marry right up to the day Noah entered the ark. They knew nothing about what was happening until the flood came and destroyed them all." (Matt. 24:37-40 AMP)

"Know ye not the friendship of the world is enmity with God"? (James 4:4 KJV) "Scripture continuously warns us concerning the "spirit of the world" and the dangers of friendship with the world's system." Harold Vaughn

We must take care not to be desensitized to the sins of this age and loose our fervor for the Lord.

We are living in dangerous times. The news media continues to broadcast injustice, robbery and murder. Our government is unstable, and the police force is not dependable. Unrest is seen worldwide.

Even our beloved planet earth is experiencing unrest. Earthquakes are rocking this world in various places. It is now time for believers to wake up from sleep. Our salvation is nearer now than when we first believed.

"The night [this present evil age] is almost gone and the day [of Christ's return] is almost here. So let us fling away the works of darkness and put on the [full] armor of light. Let us conduct ourselves properly and honorably as in the [light of] day, not in carousing and drunkenness, not in sexual promiscuity and irresponsibility, not in quarreling and jealousy. But clothe yourselves with the Lord Jesus Christ, and make no provision for [nor even think about gratifying] the flesh in regard to its improper desires." (Romans 13:12-14 AMP)

The following are excerpts from Harold Vaughn's essay: "The Spirit of The Age" Paul said in (1Cor. 2:12 KJV) "Now we have not received the spirit of the world, but the spirit which is of God." Vaughn said he feared: "We have drunk so deeply into the "spirit of the age" or "world spirit" that everything is seen as compatible with Christianity." If we desire revival in America, we must examine the thought pattern and ideas of our generation. And reject the spirit that is pulling us away from God.

Harold Vaughn's list of four attitudes of this "World's Spirit."

Tolerance

Willingness to accept feelings, habits, or beliefs that are different from our own.

The last virtue of a totally corrupt society is tolerance. A.W. Tozer wrote, "A new Decalogue has been adopted by the Neo Christians of our day, 'Thou shalt not disagree' and a new set of Beatitudes too, blessed are they that tolerate everything, for they shall not be made accountable for anything."

Pragmatism

Dealing with things sensibly and realistically in a way that is based on practical rather than theoretical considerations.

"If it works it must be right." "If it is successful it must be right." When churches are judged on their ability to draw large crowds and produce pleasant emotions pragmatism is at work.

It rejects the belief that there is absolute truth or error, right or wrong, good or evil. And defines truth as whatever is useful, meaningful, or helpful.

Hmm! What does God think about that?

Lawlessness

Not restrained or controlled by law: unruly

Lawlessness is rebellion and is the beginning of every manifestation of the world spirit. (1 Samuel 15:23 KJV) shows us the true nature of rebellion, where Samuel a prophet of God, says to Saul, "Rebellion is as the sin of witchcraft."

Saul failed to do what he had been instructed by Samuel. Partial obedience is disobedience. The spirit of rebellion is as serious as sorcery, and sorcery is the spirit of Satan. "Rebellion is the genesis of every manifestation of the world spirit. As the world backs up more and more from God, many of the churches are falling right behind the world. The spirit of rebellion is manifested in the home, the church and in the whole of society.

I'm a pastor's wife and I've heard some individuals say: "He (the Pastor) puts on his pants one leg at a time, just like me." As if to say, he's just a man. I don't have to do what he says. Truth of the matter is, if he loves God and His people, he is not just a man. He is a God man, called by God, to watch over the believer's soul. The bible says: "Obey them that have the rule over you, and submit yourselves; for they watch for your souls, as they that must give account, that they may do it with joy, and not with grief: for that is unprofitable for you." (Heb. 13:17 KJV) Church members don't give your pastors grief.

Self-Centeredness

Preoccupied with oneself and one's affairs.

Many of today's Christians have been corrupted by the passion for pleasure.

Dietrich Bonhoeffer said, "When Christ call a man, He bids him to come and die." True and everlasting happiness comes through self-denial, not self-indulgence.

Many Christians today no longer live for heaven. So the concept of detachment from this world is seldom considered, let alone practiced.

The world is after pleasure, profit, power, and privilege, and so are we!"

Bonhoeffer uses a generalization concerning Christians; we understand that not all are after pleasure, profit, power and privilege.

Contrary to popular thinking, the spirit of this age is not the spirit of God!

(Rom.12:2 KJV) tells us, "Be not conformed to this world: but be ye transformed by the renewing of your minds.

(Col. 3:2 KJV) "Set your affections on things above, not on things on the earth."

Do we reflect the image of God, or do we merely mirror the culture? Are we more like the unchanging Christ or the world which is passing away? Is our outlook humanistic or Christian? Are our world views Biblical or pagan? Are we ambassadors for God's kingdom or merely salesman in the kingdom of this world? Brethren, are we guilty of the subtle sin of worldliness?

PART FIVE

Mercy Received

"Mercy is the stuff you give to people that don't deserve it."
Joyce Meyer

MERCY

A blessing that is an act of divine favor or compassion

"The Lord smelled these (Noah's) sacrifices, and it pleased him. The Lord said to himself, "I will never again curse the earth as a way to punish people. People are evil from the time they are young, but I will never again destroy every living thing on the earth as I did this time." (Genesis 8:21 ERV)

What caused God to make such a declaration?

One man's obedience, and respect for the Almighty, caused Him to see hope in a flawed humanity.

Every day when we open our eyes and get out of bed, the Lord has extended His mercy. The air we breathe is a sign of His mercy; even though we pollute it. His mercies are new every day.

"It is of the Lord's mercies that we are not consumed, because his compassions fail not. They are new every morning: great is thy faithfulness." (Lamentations 3:22-23 KJV)

"Many people are suffering-crushed by the weight of their troubles. But the Lord is a refuge for them, a safe place they can run to. Lord those who know your name come to you for protection And when they come, you do not leave them without help." (Psalm 9:9-10 ERV)

"God makes His sun rise on those who are evil and on those who are good, and makes the rain fall on the righteous [those who are morally upright] and the unrighteous [the unrepentant, those who oppose Him]." (Matthew 5:45b AMP)

It's wonderful to know that God cares about all humanity. And "as long as the earth continues, there will always be a time for planting and a time for harvest. There will always be cold and hot, summer and winter, day and night on earth." (Genesis 8:22 ERV) It is better to know; "Surely goodness and mercy and unfailing love shall follow me all the days of my life, And I shall dwell forever [throughout all my days] in the house and in the presence of the Lord." (Psalm 23:6 AMP)

(Psalm 136:26 AMP) says: "Give thanks to the God of heaven, For His lovingkindness, (graciousness, mercy, compassion) endures forever."

Solomon said this: in (Proverbs 28:13 AMP) "He who conceals his transgressions will not prosper, But whoever confesses and turns away from his sins will find compassion and mercy."

"God is being patient with you, He doesn't want anyone to be lost. He wants everyone to change their ways and stop sinning." (2 Peter 3:9b ERV)

"Yes, God loved the world so much that he gave his only Son, so that everyone who believes in him would not be lost but have eternal life." (John 3:16 ERV)

"If we [freely] admit that we have sinned and confess our sins, He is faithful and just [true to His own nature and promises], and will forgive our sins and cleanse us continually from all unrighteousness [our wrongdoing, everything not in conformity with His will and purpose]." (1 John 1:9 AMP)

And "to as many as did receive and welcome Him, He gave the right [the authority, the privilege] to become children of God, that is to those who believe in (adhere to, trust in, and rely on) His name." (John 1:9 AMP)

Thank you, Lord for your mercy!

INVITATION TO RECEIVE CHRIST

If you have read this far in this book and realize that you need Jesus in your life, He has touched your heart. "No one can come to Me unless the Father who sent me draws him [giving him the desire to come to me]; and I will raise him up [from the dead on the last day." (John 6:44 AMP)

"If you declare with your mouth, "Jesus is Lord", and believe in your heart that God raised him from the dead, you will be saved. For it is with your heart that you believe and are justified, and it is with your mouth that you profess your faith and are saved." (Romans 10:9-10 NIV)

From your heart pray something like this: "Dear Jesus, I'm a sinner, I ask you to forgive me of my sins. I believe that you died for my sins and rose from the dead. I invite you to come into my heart and cleanse me from sin. I receive you as my Lord and Savior. Amen

If you have prayed this prayer; you have been forgive. Live for Christ. Get in a Bible believing church and have fellowship with other believers. Attend church regularly so you can grow in the knowledge of Jesus Christ. Pray every day and study your Bible.

I will be praying for you!

PART SIX

Aroma Therapy

Their fruit will be for food, and their leaves for healing.
Ezekiel 47:12 AMP

"Integrity is the essence of everything successful."
Buckminster Fuller

AROMA THERAPY

"Aromatherapy in the holistic sense is the use of natural plant extracts to promote health and well-being. Sometimes it's called essential oil therapy.

Aromatherapy uses aromatic essential oils medicinally to improve the health of the body, mind, and spirit. It enhances both physical and emotional health.

If used correctly these oils offer therapeutic benefits. But there are some precautions as well as side effects one should be aware of when using them." (www.healthline.com)

The world of advertising does not regulate the use of the word aromatherapy; so any product can be marketed as suitable. "The field is currently an unregulated and unlicensed field both for the practice of aromatherapy as well as the manufacture of aromatherapy products." (naha.org.>explore-aromatherapy>regulations)

The product can have the label and not the content. Some potential buyers may shy away from the benefit of the real thing because of false advertising. The reality is: the pure oils have been testified by many and found to be beneficial.

Appealing fragrance comes from the natural and pureness of essential oil blends.

God has given man wisdom in the natural realm to benefit the well-being of mankind. Applying these principles (standards) of pure essence can be a blessing and enlightenment in the spiritual realm?

GOD'S STANDARD

God has a standard! He will not except just anything. He has an established rule for quality, expressed in the Old and New Testaments.

We see God's standards in the Old Testament in regard to animal sacrifices.

"God required animal sacrifices to provide a temporary covering of sins and to foreshadow the perfect and complete sacrifice of Jesus Christ (Leviticus 4:35; 5:10 KJV) He commanded the nation of Israel to perform numerous sacrifices according to certain procedures prescribed by God. First, the animal had to be spotless." (http://www.gotquestions.org Why did God require animal sacrifices in the OT)

"You shall not sacrifice to the Lord your God an ox or a sheep which has a blemish or any defect, for that is a detestable thing to the Lord your God." (Deuteronomy 17:1 AMP) No creature which had any blemish was to be offered in sacrifice to God, it was a type of Christ. We are thus called to remember the perfect, pure, and spotless sacrifice of Christ. And reminded to serve God with the best of our abilities, time, and possession, or our pretended obedience will be hateful to Him. (https://www.Studylight.org Deut. 17 Matthew Henry's Complete Commentary)

God's principles have been tried and tested. These principles are found to be pure and beneficial psychologically, physically and spiritually. Just as aromas can be therapeutic, and offer benefits naturally, our aroma before God can be therapeutic and offer benefits spiritually; not just for ourselves, but for the well-being of others.

In Ezekiel the forty-seventh chapter God gave Ezekiel a vision of life-giving water coming from out of the temple as it flows it grows and everything it touches begins to flourish; this is a supernatural river. The river's purpose is to bring God's refreshing life. In verse ten it talks about an abundance of fish and we've learned the fish could represent souls. So this may refer to the many soul that will come to know Jesus through evangelism. This river shows similarities of the river that flows from God's throne in New Jerusalem (Rev. 22:1-2 KJV) It is also similar to the one mentioned by Jesus which states "Whosoever believeth in me as the scripture has said, out of his belly shall flow rivers of living water." (Jn.7:38 KJV) Jesus was speaking of the Holy Spirit which those who adheres to, trusts in and relies on Him, would receive. "Some view this passage of scripture as a description of the spiritual revival God desires to bring among his people if they will pray and prepare for God to use them to bring a flood of people into the kingdom."

(Fire Bible notes Water Coming Out From...The Temple Pg. 1467)

THERAPY

It is our responsibility to make a difference in the areas the Lord has given us. Believers are strategically placed in environments to affect change, growth and health for the kingdom. The ingredient that is so powerful to do this is God's Spirit. The Holy Spirit on the inside of a believer works outwardly. He does not cover up sin, but gets rid of its defilement. He is the pure essence and not the synthetic. He is attainable to all searching for the true quality of God. His holiness gives new life.

Don't shy away from content (the spirit of God) because of false advertising. Receive God's Spirit, learn how He works, allow Him to take the helm of your life. Reap the benefits of His leading now and into eternity.

AROMA THERAPIST

As believers we are to be effective therapist to those in need of healing.

We must humble ourselves before God. "He who habitually humbles himself (keeps a realistic self-view) will be exalted." (Luke 14:11b AMP) Knowing that it is an honor to serve God and His people. "Know and fully recognize with gratitude that the Lord Himself is God; It is He who has made us, not we ourselves [and we are His]. We are His people and the sheep of His pasture." (Psalm 100:3 AMP) He gives one wisdom and strength. "But the wisdom from above is first pure [morally and spiritually undefiled], then peace-loving [courteous, considerate], gentle, reasonable [and willing to listen], full of compassion and good fruit. It is unwavering, without [self-righteous] hypocrisy [and self-righteous guile].

Reach up to God – It is His anointing that destroys yokes in the lives of individuals. "This is the word of the Lord unto Zerubbabel, saying Not by might, nor by power, but by my spirit, saith the Lord of host." (Zechariah 4:6 KJV) "God has spoken once, twice have I heard this, That power belongs to God." (Psalm 62:11 KJV) "He giveth power to the faint; and to them that have no might he increaseth strength." (Isaiah 40:29 KJV)

We will have challenges, but the Lord will give strength to endure.

"But you will receive power and ability when the Holy Spirit comes upon you; and you will be My witnesses [to tell people about Me] both in Jerusalem and in all Judea, and Samaria, and even to the ends of the earth." (Acts 1:8 AMP)

Reach Out to humanity– Jesus told his followers: "Therefore go and make disciples of all nations baptizing them in the name of the Father and of the Son and of the Holy Spirit, and teaching them to obey everything I have commanded you. And surely, I am with you always, to the very end of the age." (Matthew 28:19-20 NIV)

"In the final instructions, Christ states the goal and responsibility of his church. They are to take his message to people of all nations and cultures. Preaching "repentance and forgiveness of sins" (Luke24:47 KJV), the promise of receiving "the gift of the Holy Spirit"(Acts 2:38 KJV) and challenging them to live in a way that is uniquely different from the corrupt world (Acts 2:40 NIV). The primary purpose of Christ's commission was to make disciples; followers of Jesus who live by his commands and are continually growing in their relationship with him."

(Fire Bible Global Study Edition ref. notes Matt. 28:19 NIV pg. 1761)

Empty Out of one's self – I have been crucified with Christ [that is, in Him I have shared His crucifixion]; it is no longer I who live, but Christ lives in me. The life I now live in the body I live by faith [by adhering to, relying on, and completely trusting] in the Son of God, who loved me and gave Himself up for me." (Galatians 2:20 AMP) *The Life of Jesus is an invaluable treasure.*

"We have this treasure from God, but we are only like clay jars that hold the treasure. This is to show that the amazing power we have is from God, not from us. We have troubles all around us, but we are not defeated. We often don't know what to do, but we don't give up. We are persecuted, but God does not leave us. We are hurt sometimes, but we are not destroyed. So we constantly experience the death of Jesus in our own bodies, but this is so that the life of Jesus can also be seen in our bodies. We are alive, but for Jesus we are always in danger of death, so that the life of Jesus can be seen in our bodies that die. So death is working in us, but the result is that life is working in you." (2 Corinthians 4:7-12 ERV)

Life has exposed you to challenges, and you've gained valuable lessons. These lessons have equipped you to be a help to someone else. To be an effective teacher one must need to have been taught. And "Experience is the Best Teacher"

Julius Caesar recorded the earliest version 'Experience is the teacher of all things,' in De Bello Civile' (c.52B.C.) en.m.wikipedia. org>wiki>Ut_est_

The people whose lives you have touched will be made better for knowing you.

SPIRITUALLY AROMATIC

I'm so grateful for the Spiritually Aromatic persons God has placed in my life.

The wonderful men and women of faith, whose life mirrored a deep love for Christ. And a resolve to share that love with me.

They were instruments in the hand of the Lord to shape me into the person I am today. Although some I didn't thank the Lord for, at the time. But later realized they also had a part in my shaping.

Apostle Paul proclaimed in (1 Corinthians 3:6-7 KJV) "I have planted, Apollos watered; but God gave the increase. So then neither is he that planteth any thing, neither he that watereth; but God that giveth the increase."

The first example of an aromatic life was my husband. A diamond in the rough, greatly valued but not at its full potential. Despite being in a backslidden state he would say, when coming to visit me; "if the Lord's will I'll be there."

He spoke of his parents being saved and explained what that meant, because at the time I had no clue. Even without Christ in his life he

Lynette Johnson

had a kind and loving demeanor. He may not have recognized it at the time, but Christ had him.

Our relationship started off as a young man I met at the Blue Chateau night club. As time progressed, he became my boyfriend and two years later my husband.

I am so honored to say that, that same young man has been my husband for over forty-five years and my pastor for over seventeen years. He is a man who loves God and His people, rising early to seek the Lord. Fasting and praying weekly for the people of God and lost humanity.

My father and mother-in-love were the next examples of a spiritual aroma. Known affectionately as mama and daddy. Daddy (Roosevelt Johnson Sr.) is a very quiet man, full of wisdom and a great provider for his family. He is a godly man and a great example of a loving father. Working hard to ensure that his nine children were housed, clothed, and fed. Instilling in them the gift of work and the blessing of providing for family. He served faithfully as a deacon in his church, being a blessing financially and using his skills for the upkeep of the building.

He worked for East Saint Louis Steel Casting Company, for twenty-nine years. After the company closed, he became an entrepreneur. As a certified electrician daddy established a business, with a second-grade education. God blessed him to use his knowledge and talents as a mainstay for his family and others in the community. These skills he imparted to several of his sons.

At the age of eighty-five he came to San Antonio Texas and wired the marque at our church. God has truly blessed him. Daddy continued to drive his car until he was ninety-four years old. He will be ninety-seven in May of 2021. He still is quick witted, and has a sharp mind.

And behind every good man is a good woman. Mother Willie Mae Johnson (affectionally known as mama) showed me so much love when I first met her. She made me feel at ease; not coming from a

112

background of holiness. She shared her testimony with me: how the Lord had healed her of seven tumors. This aroused a desire in me to want to know the God that she talked about. It was evident that she had a personal relationship with Him. Mama Johnson was always so kind and would feed me royally. The biscuits mama made would melt in your mouth! She was a great cook, who fed not only her nine children, but church members, neighbors and many others. Her compassionate heart was evident by the souls who came to know Jesus Christ through her life. She would visit the sick often and do whatever she could to help anyone. As a prayer warrior, one would find her at the church for noon day prayer service. Interceding for the sick and shut-in, her pastor, her children, the church members, the world and all who requested prayer. Always praying and glorifying her God.

The third person is my father in the Gospel: Bishop Frank Elijah Johnson. I came to know Jesus Christ as my savior under his ministry. In May 1978 I gave my life to the Lord and My Husband rededicated his life. This man of God played such a vital role in my foundation and growth in Christ. My mother who was diagnosed with lung cancer, received Christ under his ministry. When she was hurting or feeling bad, she would ask us to call Bishop Johnson, and he would pray for her without hesitation. After the call she would say "I feel better." She had confidence in the anointing on Bishop's life to heal the sick. I will never forget the night that I received the Baptism in the Holy Ghost. It was the night my mother went home to be with the Lord. Bishop Johnson prayed for me and the spirit of God flooded my soul with His presence.

He was a very generous man giving to so many untiringly. All the members received a turkey at Thanksgiving and fruit and candy at Christmas. Bishop bought chocolate candy and kept it in his office for the children. But the young ladies (me included) would visit his office for some of that yummy chocolate candy, after church service. My son Reginald had problem with cartilage in his knee and could hardly walk. Bishop Johnson prayed for him and the Lord healed his body. Four of our eight children were born under his ministry. When Joseph (my husband) went to Korea on a remote tour, Bishop and Mother Johnson made sure that my children and I didn't need for anything. One time I had car trouble; Bishop and Elder McMillon came to the house and fixed the car. He has one natural son but was a father figure to so many others. I can't talk about Bishop without saying something about the great woman of God who stood by his side for 66 year until his demise. Mother Thelma Johnson has a sweet gentle spirit. She always seemed so calm and in control. I believed that calmness was due to her faith and confidence in God, who would work all things together for her good. Mother is a wonderful example of a godly woman and a beautiful pastor's wife. When my husband got an assignment to the Philippines, I wrote to Mother Johnson after he started pastoring. I asked her what should I do to be a good pastor's wife? Mother sent me a book to help me, which I still have. It's entitled "So You're the Pastor's Wife" by Ruth Hollinger Senter. I opened the book and the last paragraph in the preface read: "And when all is said and done, what really matters is not to whom we are married or what roles we happen to fill in life, but how we respond to the life that God has set before us. Herein lies the thread that draws us together as wives in the process of learning godlike responses to the tension points of life." She wrote on the inside of the book: "May God richly Bless you. You will make a Great Pastor's Wife April 16, 1985 Love Sis. Thelma Johnson." The book was a blessing in my life and those words from Mother was a great encouragement to me. I felt and still feel that Mother Thelma Johnson is a perfect pastor's wife and one to emulate.

After all that has been said: The question remains what kind of example do you want to be? Do you want to live your life so that it is beneficial to others?

Would you like to make God smile?

You can start right now!

Endeavor to be a Sweet Aroma to God!

SCRIPTURE TRANSLATION
USED IN MANUSCRIPT

American Standard Version - ASV
Amplified Bible – AMP
Easy-to Read Version – ERV
English Standard Version - ESV
God's Word Translation – GW
Holman Christian Standard Bible - HCSB
King James Version – KJV
New International Version – NIV
New Life Version - NLV
New Living Translation – NLT
The Message – MSG

Printed in the United States
by Baker & Taylor Publisher Services